D1431472

# THE Magic CAKE

## *The Seven Ingredients*
### of a Relationship-Ready Person

# The Magic Cake

## The seven ingredients
## of a relationship-ready person

Jennifer Lehr MFT

**The Magic Cake**

Copyright© 2015 by Jennifer Lehr MFT

ALL RIGHTS RESERVED.

This publication may not be reproduced, stored, or transmitted in whole or in part, in any form or by any means, electronic, mechanical, or otherwise, without prior written consent from the publisher and author. Brief quotations may be included in a review.

The information in this book is based on the author's opinion, knowledge, and experience. The publisher and author will not be held liable for the use or misuse of the information contained herein.

**Note:** Although much of this book is autobiographical, the stories of couples are composites of multiple couples with names and details changed.

Cover design by Joy A. Miller at FiveJsDesign.com

Printed in the United States of America

First Printing, 2015

ISBN 978-0-9963860-0-5

Jennifer Lehr MFT Press
P.O. Box 507
Olga, WA 98279

www.jenniferlehrmft.com

# Table of Contents

# Preface

**We often don't look at what we bring to the relational table. Would you choose yourself? Why? Why not?**

Many relationship self-help books aid you in deciphering how to "get" the person you want. Few relationship self-help books work on the principal of manifesting and the law of attraction—that who you are determines who comes into your life. "Getting" the relationship you want is not like fishing for a big catch. It is like creating a beautiful garden (yourself) that others want to hang out in with you. This book will challenge you to make yourself into a relationship-ready person.

This book will help you do so by guiding you to:

1. Recognize the qualities needed for a successful relationship.

2. Identify the areas of your life to address in order to have that successful relationship.

3. Begin to make those changes so that you can have the relationship of your dreams.

You may or may not already be in a relationship. It doesn't matter. You can learn about these seven ingredients while single or if you are already in a partnership.

# Introduction

Relationships are among the biggest challenges any of us encounter in our lives. They are the fabric of our lives, the weave within which we live. They can lift us to feelings of glory, or cause us to crash into despair. They simply aren't easy. Many of us don't know what makes them survive or fail or why some have successful relationships and others do not.

We live in an age of quick, easy, and disposable. But in the world of relationships, spiritual growth, and maturing into wisdom, there aren't any quick fixes. A relationship isn't fast food. It is a slow process of learning to connect and love fully. For most of us, this process of learning occurs over our entire lifetime. It is my hope that this book will help you sort through the qualities that can make or break a relationship, allow you to develop the ones you need, and bring into your life the relationship of your dreams.

# Part 1
# The Overview

# Chapter 1

## What Are Your Dreams?
## What Is Your Reality?

Who hasn't dreamed of someone being there for us, of cuddling soft skin between silky sheets, of warm hugs and kisses and the feeling of being understood and special? Who hasn't craved the sense of leaning back into a relationship that is completely safe and supportive? What about the exhilaration of love and fun and exciting sex? Who doesn't want to grow old with your own true love?

And who hasn't at some point experienced the heartbreak of feeling misunderstood, lied to, discounted, or just not special? Some of us have experienced decay creeping into a relationship as conflict and discordant needs paralyze our ability to keep our hearts open, and we feel a sad distance that cannot be bridged. Others have felt

the pain of picking someone who could not go the distance or open up their heart enough to stay connected.

What starts as the glorious feeling of being in love, can so easily fall apart. It is easy to lose our way on the path of building a relationship because we simply haven't been taught how. But it is possible to participate in the magic of creating a beautiful relationship.

Between the exhilaration of love and the distress of conflict lies an open field: a place to explore, frolic, struggle, and grow. This is where magic and work—persistence, focus, and effort—hold hands.

Much of this work is just being brave enough to take an honest look at our own selves.

No matter what your experience has been, most of us want a lasting love. If we are willing to enter the place where magic and work intertwine, we can have a love that builds, grows and sustains itself.

## My Story

Why listen to me? What do I know about getting relationship-ready? As they say, the proof is in the pudding. I wrote this book because learning how to have a great relationship has been a major focus of my life. And I've spent plenty of time feeling stuck in relationship dynamics that I did not know how to change.

I remember as a teenager telling myself I would never get married. Those earlier years were difficult for me. I had big wounds around relationships with people, primarily due to my relationships with my parents. Our family dynamics were stressful, and our household was frequently filled with fear, anger and criticism. I found solace with our pets and the animals I grew up with on our farm. But like most everyone else, I craved love and connection with people and wanted a great relationship in my life. Because of the difficult start I had in relating to others, I found myself in some *bad* relationships. These relationships (including my first marriage) showed me my weaknesses and caused me to tackle this part of my life.

I eventually ended that difficult marriage and went through a divorce so painful it felt like it would kill me. By the time I got through that trauma, I was desperate to find somebody who would look me in the eye with kindness and enjoy just being and connecting with me. And it happened. My second marriage is fulfilling and safe. I'm situated firmly in a wonderful life with a man I love and with whom I can work out any challenges. My relationship with my husband is one of the joys of my life.

Through this journey, I discovered that we are powerful beings and can change our own lives; we can learn to become that person who has a great, true-love relationship. The process might not be easy and will probably require some soul searching and even some life changes. But I can't think of one good reason not to do this. Fifty years from now, you might look back with regret and say "I wish I had done what it took;" or you could say, "I'm so glad I tackled this challenge and was able to live my life fully and experience this love."

In the process of learning about relationships first hand, I decided to become a psychotherapist. After years of training and self-improvement, I've had the privilege of guiding others in stepping into the magic of their lives and relationships.

I've also created and authored WeConcile®, an online program to help couples. You can read more about WeConcile at the end of this book or visit our website. *www.jenniferlehrmft.com/ weconcile/*

# Chapter 2

## The Vision

Once upon a time, there lived a princess. She had a good life; she loved her parents and siblings, but she was lonely. She was hungry for something. She wanted to feel complete. She wanted love. She dreamed of her prince charming. And while she dreamed, she dated and dated. She hoped and hoped. She waited and waited. One day, he finally arrived on his white horse. They fell in love and rode off into the sunset, and lived happily ever after—or so she hoped.

This is the romantic myth we have grown up with, and a dream many of us still have. It is an image of harmony and fulfillment—of manifested magic. The trouble is, as we all know, it isn't this simple. The vision of a happy relationship is only the first step; for without the right tools, we cannot create a sustainable relationship.

Relationships are complicated and challenging. The person we fell in love with will sooner or later disappoint us, and we will disappoint them. Maybe they will not get along with one of our parents and refuse to spend holidays with them, or they will stay out late with friends without calling. Or it could be something much more serious. Whatever it is, disappointment happens in every relationship.

While some couples divorce or limp along for years, others are able to create a strong relationship despite these disappointments. Gaining the skills needed takes work and is often difficult. It requires digging deep into who we are and understanding our limitations, our wounds, and our needs. Yet engaging in a successful relationship is also like making a cake. We are the ingredients. We determine what our cake is made of. As we add more and more of ourselves, our cake gets even more delicious!

You might ask why. Why was my first marriage so difficult and my second one so much easier and more nourishing? I don't want to make it all my first husband's fault, although *some* of it was. He didn't like talking about his feelings. He didn't like being vulnerable; for him it was easier to get angry or shut down. He wasn't comfortable with many emotions—especially mine. My second husband is a connector. And he is someone who is willing to learn to do what it takes to make our relationship work.

But the bottom line is that I changed a lot over the years I was in my first marriage. The changes I made enabled me to attract a very different kind of person the next time around. I was ready to pick someone better suited for me. I had learned a lot about relationships over the twenty-five years since my very first romantic relationship. (Okay, so it took me a long time.) I was finally relationship-ready, and I wasn't going accept a person who wasn't able to go the distance with me.

But back to making a magic cake.

# Chapter 3

## Making a Magic Cake

I learned to bake and cook as a child. Baking is second nature to me. Easy, fun, rewarding—just like relating is for me now most of the time, though there are always challenges and new things to learn.

When you make a cake, you first find a recipe, something yummy. You decide what flavor and type of cake you like. This is the envisioning part, like when you imagine your ideal relationship or partner.

Then you get your cake pan out and turn on the oven. You gather the ingredients you have on hand or go shopping to get them. You measure them, put them together, and mix them. This is where you do the work of making the cake.

You may taste the uncooked cake batter still in the bowl. It tastes good, but it isn't a cake. You put your cake in the oven and clean up the mess in the kitchen. (There's a mess if you're like me!) The fragrance of the baking cake fills the room. There's an alchemy that occurs as the ingredients and heat come together to form something new—something magical. Flour, sugar, eggs, and oil transform into a light, delicious cake. When the cake is ready, you take it out, let it cool, cut into it, and take a big bite. YUM. This is the good part—where the vision and the work merge into something new and beautiful.

And then soon, you'll do it all over again. Over time, you will learn to make a pretty mean cake. You have fewer accidents. You start to veer from the recipe. You experiment. You try new flavors. You invent your own. Making a cake becomes more creative. It becomes easier, more fun, and more satisfying. Like everything in life, creating something beautiful is a process, not an event.

But making a cake isn't all easy fun. Sometimes in the middle of it, everything is a mess. There is egg on the ceiling, batter on the walls, and dirty dishes piled on every counter. During this stage of cake-making, our hope may wane. Is this mess really going to turn into something? This is the relational stage many of us find ourselves in. We don't understand that the process of transformation can be frustrating, messy, or uncomfortable. We don't understand why we are having what seems like the same fight yet again. We don't understand why we hurt so much. We don't understand how to get from the mixing bowl to the cake.

## What is Relationship-Ready?

How does this shift from difficult to joyful happen in a relationship? It starts with being *relationship-ready*. This means you have developed the ingredients in yourself that allow you to be in touch with the magic of you, which is what makes making a magic cake possible at all.

This is what you are going to learn in this book—becoming *relationship-ready* and stepping into the magic of who you are.

Being *relationship-ready* includes being able to pick a person who is willing to roll up his or her sleeves and step into the kitchen with us. It means having the attitude that we can and must learn from our relationships. It means accepting that every relationship requires work and that conflict is natural. It means knowing that making a cake—even a magic one, can be messy.

And it's about understanding what *manifestation* means. For something to manifest, the conditions must be right. A seed cannot sprout without soil and water. It cannot grow without the sun. For a fantastic relationship (one that has moved beyond the initial haze of being in love), there are conditions that are needed. You are going to be learning about those "conditions" as we continue in the following chapters.

# Chapter 4

## The Fairy Tale

Let's start by looking at the concept of fairy tales, which are stories that illuminate psychological states of being. In a fairy tale about true love, we are looking at an internal state of *completion*. We tend to literalize this and think it means our unhappiness or yearning will be "fixed" by another. But this isn't what actually happens. Instead, through the process of tackling our lives and our own unfinished psychological, spiritual, and emotional rough spots, we become more complete. This process can be done with a willing partner, which is what relationships are all about—growth—in the context of connection, support, and love. That doesn't mean being in a safe, connected relationship isn't something worth yearning for, or that it isn't incredibly valuable. It means a relationship isn't a substitute for our own inner growth. Instead, it can often be a catalyst.

With that said, looking beyond the fantasy fairy tale where falling in love is the answer, we can learn several things.

First, in order to find "the one" or to make it work with the one we already have, we need to look at ourselves. There are reasons we've been drawn to our partner or past partners. If we take a hard look, we usually will find a deeper emotional pattern in our previous failed relationships (both romantic and platonic).

Second, falling in love is the initial glue, but it does not ensure the magic cake will be made. For you (and your partner, if you have one) to make the magic cake and take this journey, it will require lots of strength, courage, vulnerability, and learning as you develop new tools and skills.

Instead of pushing all the difficult stuff that occurs between two people under the rug, we learn to take it out, look at it, talk about it, and eventually be okay and love each other despite it. The benefit of this journey is both having a love that works *and* learning to become a healthier, more developed person and partner.

As we change, our world transforms, including our relationships. This is the power each of us has. Like magic, our world literally becomes different, filled with light and love in ways that we could not even imagine.

# Chapter 5

## The Principle of Manifestation

Are you familiar with the principle of manifestation? This is important so I will explain it here.

We manifest constantly. Our thoughts, beliefs, and feelings create an energy flow within and around us. This energy attracts whatever we need to evolve to a higher state. So if you're thinking, "nothing ever works out for me," then your energy attracts the kind of experience that reinforces this belief that you already have. And it's not an experience that will "take away" this belief; you have to do that yourself.

The opposite experience occurs when we think, feel, and believe higher-vibration thoughts like, "I love my life." When we think and

feel those kinds of thoughts, we radiate the energy of confidence and gratitude, which attracts positive experiences into our lives. Each thought, feeling, and belief we have affects our energy, which in turn manifests our experiences. We create our own reality. Because much of our thinking, feeling, and believing is unconscious, we are often not aware of the beliefs that we are projecting and the reality that we are creating.

Changing our beliefs is not as simple as telling ourselves something positive that we don't really believe, because feelings, beliefs, and thoughts exist as deep-rooted patterns that do not dissolve easily. Pretending we have the right beliefs won't work. There is no way to fake this. How we respond to our reality shows us what our beliefs are. We project our reality. This means we have to identify our real beliefs before we can change them.

This doesn't necessarily mean that if you have a great life, then you already have the right beliefs. (This is a complicated subject that I am not going to address fully here.) But how you respond to your reality shows what your beliefs are. Take Nelson Mandela as an example. He was able to hold onto his beliefs and become an undeniable force for positive change, despite his difficult circumstances. His internal stance was a more important reality for him than his outer circumstances. His inner stance had a huge impact on his experience of reality and eventually had an enormous impact on the world.

Here is another way to look at this. As humans, we attract challenges. Our challenges have the potential to help us grow and become more complete, developed, and evolved. But challenges require an investment. The more we put in, the more bountiful and beautiful the results.

Another example: If you are someone who has trouble saying no, you may draw someone in who pushes you around, so you have to learn how to say no. We attract according to who we are energetically. This means if we have a blind spot, we manifest someone who fits right into that blind spot—as a trigger—until we are no longer blind in this area.

## Are You Similar to Judy?

Judy kept picking boyfriends who had addictions. They continually broke her trust as their addictions sabotaged the needs of their relationship. These boyfriends lied and broke promises because getting a quick fix was more important to them than being there for her.

Judy was heartbroken after her current boyfriend Sam disappointed her yet again. She decided she'd had enough of this, so she began to look at what was causing this pattern. When she saw that she was afraid of confrontation—among other things—she rolled up her sleeves and faced some fears. She started behaving

differently and began telling others what she felt and thought. She realized it wasn't okay when others broke their word to her. Instead of trying to change others, she decided she was worth being treated well. As a result, she left friendships that weren't supportive. In short, she chose to change.

As Judy became empowered, she chose not to date men who had "red flag" behaviors; and it was only after that decision that she met *the one*. They fell in love. Six months later, conflicts began to emerge as they do in all relationships. This is when their real journey began, and together they took on the task of learning how to make a magic cake.

# Chapter 6

## The Ingredients

Let's see *if* and *how* we are stopping ourselves from our perfect love and change that. We start by looking at ourselves. We *all* have flawed or undeveloped ways of being in our relationships. We've all hurt others, unintentionally or not. We've all put up with bad behavior or hoped that something would work that didn't have a chance. Me, too. I've had bad breakups and emotional outbursts, not stood up for myself when I should have, accepted unacceptable behavior, and had delusions about a partner. Relationship mishaps are part of our path of understanding what we need. These mishaps give us opportunities to make changes that will allow us to manifest a great relationship.

Instead of believing it's the other person's fault, or staying in a relationship that is doomed, let's practice putting on our relationship glasses to see more clearly what's going on.

1. Am I doing something that's causing a problem?

2. Have I picked someone who won't ever step up to the relational mixing bowl with me?

3. Do we each just need more tools so we can make our magic cake together?

These are three big questions and aspects of our relationship-ready path: looking at what needs to be developed in ourselves, looking at whom we've picked, and looking at what we need to learn in order to stay together.

As we become more aligned with our best relational selves, either our current relationship will grow and evolve or we will draw in someone new who better matches the new person we have become. We no longer accept "not good enough." At the same time, we have increasing compassion and patience for our partner's difficulties and struggles and for our relationship's growing pains. There is a tricky line between working with someone else's faults, as well as our own, versus accepting what is not good enough. Navigating this line teaches us wisdom. We don't come to our partners perfect, nor do our partners come to us perfect. But in the process of being in a growing relationship, we become more perfect for each other.

I'm going to identify some of the ingredients that are essential to being *relationship-ready*. These qualities or ingredients allow us to be whole. In a sense, these ingredients are the conditions or scaffolding for love. They are structures that allow love to be present. Just as a cake relies on flour, egg, sugar, and oil to form an entirely new substance with its own flavor, aroma, and texture, these ingredients allow love to manifest in our relationship. As we do the work of developing and integrating these ingredients in ourselves, they can work their magic and allow our magic cake to rise and our relationship to blossom.

These relationship-ready ingredients will allow us to provide support and nurturing for our partners (and ourselves). If we're not in a relationship, these ingredients will enable us to manifest someone who has similar qualities: someone who is also *relationship-ready*.

What does a *relationship-ready* person look like? I'll use myself as an example. Here are the ingredients.

## Safety

I remember when I didn't feel comfortable with myself. I was shy. I didn't know what to talk about. I didn't know if I would be able to support myself, or what my future would be. I didn't like dating. I was afraid of navigating through the world, of standing up for myself. I was afraid . . . of being me. My fears and insecurities left me likely to latch onto someone who wasn't right, which I did—more than once. I began to examine my patterns and to identify places where I got stuck. And I worked hard to change myself.

Today I feel comfortable and safe with myself. I trust myself, and

my friends trust me. I feel competent in terms of getting around in this world and am capable of taking care of myself. The glass of my life is half full, not half empty. I enjoy and play in my relationships. I am on the same team with my partner and friends; together we figure out how to resolve conflicts. I enjoy my life because I have an internal sense of safety.

## Accountability

I used to be too accountable. I took care of too much. I felt responsible for everything, even things I had no control over. I worried about so much; I *had* to make sure that everything was taken care of and that everyone else felt okay and was happy. I had to be perfect, but I tended to pick boyfriends who weren't nearly as accountable as I was. I did way too much in our relationships while they did way too little. My relationships were out of balance.

My history of being too accountable comes from growing up in a family where almost everyone walked on eggshells. There was a lot of rage in my family, and I learned to be very careful and to make sure everyone else was okay. If I took care of them (instead of myself), then blow-ups were less likely. This training in over-responsibility and over-accountability did not serve me in my intimate relationships.

Of course, the flip side of this is I became willing to look at myself. Eventually, I learned that my imperfections were not something to be ashamed of, but part of my unique humanness and also a place to focus and grow. I learned that as my imperfections emerged, I could address them and become a better person and partner. I'm still a highly accountable person, but I don't step into my partner's life and fix what is his to take care of.

Being accountable means that I "own" my stuff and can separate it from your stuff. This means that my partner doesn't have to agree with me on everything. Sometimes this means I compromise or shift my position. Sometimes it means I stand firm and do not give in. It almost always means that we talk about it.

## Empowerment

I remember when I put up with all kinds of bad behavior from others. It was as if I was a servant and other people could treat me however they wanted. I just didn't know I could stand up for myself, or when I did, I waited until my resentment had built up so much that my behavior was pretty inappropriate. I didn't have a good sense of my value.

Now I respect myself. I respect others too. I don't put up with bad behavior. When somebody behaves badly towards me and isn't capable of apologizing and taking responsibility for what they did, that relationship is over. I also don't engage in bad behavior myself—or if I do, I apologize and make amends as soon as I realize I have crossed a line. I have become much more balanced and empowered, and so are the people I now manifest in my life.

## Empathy

Like most babies, I started with an open heart. Yet sometime after my sister was born (she is about eighteen months younger than me), I crawled into her crib and bit her on the cheek. My mother now had her hands full with my sister and brother—twins. The full-time attention that undoubtedly had been doted on me evaporated, and I must have been overcome with jealousy.

My experience is that love and empathy flow naturally from me until something difficult occurs. I have always been good at seeing both sides of a situation, unless I was the one who was hurt. That's when I found my heart closing off. I felt like it was the other person's fault. I had trouble understanding his or her very different perspective.

Jealousy and other ways of closing our hearts (resentment, anger, blame, judgment, etc.) are part of our human experiences. But we can learn to transcend these feelings and attitudes.

Over the years, even when I have been upset myself, I have learned how to put myself in the shoes of other people. I continue to get better at this. With my husband, I've learned to see his vulnerabilities and fears with *empathy*. I've learned to keep my heart more open, even when I feel challenged. I've learned to see the part of others that is wounded or hurt and needs my empathy and compassion. Love doesn't exist without empathy and compassion. This kind of love is the guiding principal in my relationship with others and my relationship with myself.

## Vulnerable Communication

When I was growing up in my family, I didn't know how to communicate with vulnerability. At times, these relationships erupted into screaming and yelling. While this was a release of feelings, we didn't talk about or share our emotions in a constructive manner. To me, it seemed the other person wasn't interested in how I felt. Feelings just weren't part of our family dialog. Instead, we talked about ideas and logistics. I don't think I ever talked about my feelings growing up, although I expressed them. (I cried a lot.) But I had a journal, and I wrote my feelings there. This kept me connected to the feeling part of myself. I didn't communicate with my family those vulnerable feelings I was writing down; the safe atmosphere needed for that didn't exist. In my early relationships, I couldn't let myself be unguarded with my partners. Even the words "I love you" were too vulnerable to say out loud.

All of that changed. I continued to write, and this opened up my feelings more and more. I went to therapy and talked about what I was experiencing. I eventually went back to school for my masters in psychology and began to work as a psychotherapist. I stepped fully into the world of emotions and the communication of them. Feelings became my new home, and vulnerable communication became the way to solve all kinds of relational problems. As my clients opened up about their vulnerable feelings, their deep lives, their disappointments, hurts, hopes and fears, they began to nourish that part of themselves. They began to connect to, understand, and nurture their deeper selves. They began to grow, just as I had.

Now I communicate honestly and vulnerably with people I am close to, even if it feels risky because I know love is only a fantasy if I don't share my true self. I have the ability to listen. I want to hear my partner's stories and tell him mine because I want to know him and share with him. And he wants to hear my stories and tell me his because he wants to know me and share with me. As we come to know each other more fully, our relationship becomes closer and closer. Our hearts connect through our vulnerabilities, and we choose to behave in a loving manner more frequently. When we hit a snag, we have new tools and new bridges between us, and we work it out much more quickly.

## Insight

When I was younger, I felt lost and confused about many of my inner experiences. I didn't have a clear understanding of myself. I hadn't yet learned to "see into myself" with clarity. If I was worried about something, I didn't know if I was scared, or if my intuition was trying to tell me something. This freaked me out even more because I felt like I couldn't guide myself. I couldn't rely on myself to navigate through my life because I had so much confusion and anxiety. As a result, my feelings were volatile. One minute I could be laughing and the next minute crying.

When I was twenty-nine, my life hit rock bottom because of a very difficult relationship I was in. I made a decision to get help and learn about what was happening inside of me, and my focus shifted more to my internal world. I began to understand the different parts of me

# The Ingredients

and see them more clearly. I saw my fear, my grief, and my shame. I saw my anger and my intuition. I saw my joy and my excitement. As I began to unlock the parts of me that had been pushed down, I began to remember difficult events from my childhood I had forgotten. I began to understand my thoughts and feelings and know why I experienced them. I slowly became less reactive and learned to manage my emotions instead of being hijacked by them.

As my insight increased, I was able to discern and follow the guidance my life was giving me. I had moments of clarity and knowing. For example, when it was time to pick a graduate school, I looked at a list of schools; my eyes were drawn to one school. I knew that was the school for me. I applied, got in, loved it, and never looked back. My vision of my life got stronger and clearer. I was able to look back at my past and see who I had been and what had actually occurred. I also began to see my relationships more comprehensively. Instead of feeling confused about conflicts, I could see the deeper story and the needs that were sparking the flames.

My self-understanding is like a compass that points me in the right direction and allows me to navigate through my life. It allows my relationships to work. When something bothers me, I take the time to see into the complexity and identify what each of us are struggling with. This allows for the issue to be talked about and resolved.

## Magic

As a child, teenager, and young adult, there wasn't a lot of magic in my life. Instead, there was a lot of stress in my family. I was anxious and depressed during these years. I knew there was such a thing as magic, but I didn't know how to find it for myself. I was essentially on a search, trying to find myself and the magic of my life.

I did find my magic eventually. Now as I look back over my life, I can easily see the magic of my path. I see the bigger picture and what I learned through the difficult chapters and challenges. Those struggles were actually gifts, and now I understand what each chapter taught me and how I changed. I have also found magic in my relationship. I had never believed *the one* was out there for me. But he was . . . and is.

I have become somebody willing to stretch because I want to reach all of me. I want to live my full potential. I know that avoiding the challenges my life gives me will keep me smaller, and tackling them will open my life up to more possibility. I am willing to do whatever it takes for me to continue to step fully into my magical life and to keep my relationship magical. I know my path is a path of magic. Yours can be, too.

# Chapter 7

## Making the Cake Light

You've read about the seven essential ingredients needed to make a magic cake and become relationship ready. Which of these ingredients are your strong points or easy for you? Which ingredients do you find more difficult or elusive?

The ingredients that are more difficult for you will point to where you need more focus to get 100% relationship-ready. Your strong points are areas where your life is already solid. We are going to go through each of the ingredients in greater detail, so you understand them and have them available as you make your magic cake.

Whipped into the batter are some areas of focus that will increase your understanding of each of your ingredients and enable you to

make the changes needed to manifest your desires. These areas of focus add air to your cake, making it light and filled with love, understanding, and acceptance. You don't need to identify these specific areas of focus, just know that they are in the following pages to guide you. These areas of focus are:

## ˙Needs

Human love includes needs. Each of the seven ingredients is a human need. We *need* safety, accountability, empowerment, empathy, vulnerable communication, insight, and magic in our relationships and ourselves. If we didn't have needs, we would be like robots instead of the sensitive and tender beings we are.

## Inspiration and Vision

Vision is a picture or image of where you are headed. Inspiration beckons us and makes each of us want to get to that vision. Both of these show how each ingredient will help us. They breathe life, love, and beauty into us and beckon us to our future. It is our vision of our beautiful relationship that helps get us through the hard times.

## Wounds and Challenges

A wound or challenge is what may be hindering your ability to integrate this ingredient into your life. This is where it is essential to develop an ingredient or possibly heal. There will be no delicious cake if an ingredient is missing or spoiled.

## Self-Evaluation

Self-evaluation is analyzing where *you* are in terms of having developed this ingredient. This will enable you to know what you need to focus on the most and what isn't an issue for you. Self-evaluation means asking the hard questions, which isn't always fun or easy. But it is the best way to get a clear picture of where you are with each of the seven ingredients.

As you get to the self-evaluation questions for each of the seven ingredients, get some paper—or better yet, a notebook—and write down your answers to each question. Writing down your answers will give you the space to analyze, think, and even dream. It will allow you to remember who you were before you began to tackle these parts of yourself. It will allow you see how much progress you make.

If the questions seem too left brained or daunting for you, another way to self-evaluate is by getting in touch with your inner images. You can simply close your eyes and focus on the general idea offered and allow a thought, feeling, or image to emerge. Some people enjoy this form of self-evaluation more.

## How

How are you going to make this change and become your best relational self? I'll provide information on ways to begin to reinforce and develop this ingredient as effectively as possible. The "how" is part of the map. Maps help us get to our destination.

## Exercises

The exercises build on the how. You will get a specific exercise or two to create more of this ingredient in your life. Make sure you do these exercises—you'll stretch, you'll learn, you'll grow, you'll become more relationship-ready—and you will like yourself better.

## Make Your Journey Fun!

You now have an overview of the journey ahead. You are about to roll up your sleeves and step up to your mixing bowl. You are headed down the path to that fantastic person who can manifest a great relationship and become the person you have always wanted to be.

Let your journey be fun. Smell the roses along the way. The process of getting somewhere is like traveling. Every moment of the journey is special. Staying focused on the gifts in the present will keep you alive to what is. If your journey is all about the end result and not about enjoying the process, you are setting yourself up for a lot of wasted time as you miss the opportunities in each moment. Even the challenging moments of our journey have gifts. Staying present and in the moment will allow you to see those gifts more easily.

There are many people in the world who don't have this opportunity. They may have been born into poverty, denied an education, put into a factory to work as a child, or forced into an arranged marriage when they were twelve. That isn't you. You are one of the lucky ones who can choose to make the most of your life. You have the power to manifest. You have the power to make your dreams come true.

# Part 2
# The Recipe

# Chapter 8

## Ingredient One: Safety

**I feel safe in the world and comfortable with myself.**

---

I trust myself and am competent navigating my world. I am capable of taking care of myself, and my personal sense of safety allows for optimism. Because I trust myself, I can enjoy and play in my relationships. The people I pick to be with are safe for me.

Breathe in the feeling of having no fear or worries and knowing that no matter what happens in your life, you can handle it. You'll be okay. You feel so safe, in fact, that it is effortless to be a teammate and share with your partner. You have each other's backs. You see the world through the lens of abundance rather than scarcity. Breathe

that feeling in deeply. Let it take root in you. It is a fantastic place to be. It can be your future.

## How Much Safety Do You Need?

Safety is very important for me. I need to know I can trust myself. I need to know I can trust my husband in numerous ways. I need to know that I am going to survive physically and emotionally. Emotional safety means that my partner is available, engaged, and accessible to me and that I can count on him. He doesn't shut down or start yelling, and I'm not walking on eggshells.

I even need to believe that no matter what happens in my life, I can handle it, and it makes sense. Or that if I die, my soul doesn't. It makes me feel safe to believe that whatever I do now (in terms of growth and taking on the challenges of my life), I won't have to do later. Different people desire different levels of risk. Some people thrive on risk although even people who thrive on risk want safety in their close relationships.

Connected fulfilling relationships require safety and may not survive if we do not recognize how interdependent we are, how primal our feelings and how strong our need for safety. We want to know we are on the same team. We want to know our partners are there for us, and they want to know we are there for them. Safety allows us to relax, reach out, connect, communicate, share, play, love, and enjoy each other.

## Ingredient One: Safety

### Hush Little Baby

Are you responsive to me?  Look at any group of things — how the trees grow as a community in the forest, their roots entwined, a flock of birds that flies together in formation, each attuned to the movement of the group, a mother holding her child.  We live and breathe relationship and responsiveness.  Responsiveness creates safety.  Is my partner responding to me — or reacting?  Does it seem as if my world is responsive to my efforts?  Did my mother hold me close and soothe me?

The lyrics of "Hush Little Baby," paint the picture of attunement and responsiveness.  (The author and date of origin are unknown.) The little baby being sung to undoubtedly feels safe: to be crooned to, to be soothed, and to be loved.

Hush, little baby, don't say a word,

Mama's gonna buy you a mockingbird.

If that mockingbird don't sing,

Mama's gonna buy you a diamond ring

If that diamond turns to brass,

Mama's gonna buy you a looking glass.

If that looking glass gets broke,

Mama's gonna buy you a billy goat,

If that billy goat don't pull,

Mama's gonna buy you a cart and a bull.

If that cart and bull tip over,

Mama's gonna buy you a dog named Rover.

If that dog named Rover don't bark,

Mama's gonna buy you a horse and a cart.

If that horse and cart fall down,

you'll still be the sweetest little baby in town.

When you read these words you can feel that somebody is looking out for this little baby. The message of this lullaby is that no matter what, Mama is there for you and will take care of you. This is the safety that we all crave.

## Do You Feel Safe?

We aren't always able to feel safe, either physically or emotionally. We live in a world that is at times precarious, unpredictable, and painful. People and pets we love die. People we trust betray us. Accidents and unforeseen events occur. Our hearts can be broken. It can be scary to be here.

## Ingredient One: Safety

When we don't feel safe, we worry or feel anxious. We can be stressed about real situations in our lives that threaten our physical survival. We may be emotionally scarred from our past, and when those hurts are triggered, we lose our equilibrium. When we don't feel safe, we often over-control or hide ourselves. Our relationships falter. If we are stressed, we need more support and may have more trouble supporting our partner. We may be more easily on edge.

Sometimes we channel our anxiety into overdoing, over-striving or perfectionism. Over-striving means we *must* make something happen, or we feel that we will not be okay. Instead of caring for ourselves, we tell ourselves we are not safe or okay unless something specific happens. We believe that if we don't get into the right college, get the right job, or find the right relationship, we aren't okay or secure. We push and push. Our self-environment isn't nurturing because we aren't nurturing ourselves. The *thing*, whatever it is, becomes our focus. Relationships don't do well in this kind of environment. Remember, worrying is different than planning. Worrying usually doesn't get you anywhere positive unless it is a trigger to action.

I have a history of anxiety, worry, and early childhood trauma. I worried that I would make a mistake or not make the right choice. My mind would spin and spin, and I could get lost in fearful thoughts. This was so uncomfortable—painful actually. I learned to confront my fears and change my thoughts. Now when anxiety arises, I stop myself. I tell myself I will be okay, or that I can handle whatever is bothering me. Usually I am successful with this. When I am not, it is time for me to talk to someone and get support.

Because much of what we do in our relationships stems from coping mechanisms learned in our early family dynamics, it is important to look at how our family history affects our sense of safety. If we have emotional scars or places where we do not feel safe emotionally, we can react in ways that cause our partner to feel unsafe.

There are countless things that can cause emotional scars.

- Did one of your parents lack empathy or express rage?

- Was one of them was an alcoholic or untrustworthy?

- Did they have a messy divorce?

- Did they neglect to set boundaries?

- Did you experience trauma as a child?

If you experienced trauma as a child and it has impacted your sense of safety in a relationship, you can read more about how trauma impacts relationships in the following article, *"How Past Trauma Impacts Current Relationships." [www.jenniferlehrmft. com/?p=243]*

How were you impacted? How did you protect yourself? Did you withdraw, get angry, or react in another way? Whatever you did, it was because you needed to survive, and you needed to feel safe. Some of your old survival techniques may be impairing your current intimacy skills.

Common behaviors that create feelings of not being safe include:

- Not being able to take care of ourselves.

- Not being able to stand up for ourselves or putting up with abusive behavior.

- Hysterical or out of control behavior.

- Addictions or affairs.

- Cheating, lying, or abusive behavior, including criticism.

- Giving the silent treatment, withdrawing, or not listening.

- Blaming or resenting.

- Controlling behavior.

- Putting "I" over "We."

- Reacting intensely when upset and "sweeping it under the rug" when the conflict "blows over."

- Not being available or not acting interested.

- Hiding by not being transparent or by not showing or sharing ourselves.

- Not caring or connecting.

## Evaluate Your Sense of Safety

Think about your sense of safety in your life. Do you feel safe within your own being? Do you feel safe in your relationships?

What kind of life will you have if you don't feel safe? Grab your notebook and write about your sense of safety. You can use the following questions as a guide.

Or if you prefer, skip the following questions. Instead, close your eyes and think about safety. Imagine feeling completely safe. You might get an image or a feeling. Write about whatever comes up for you.

---

- Are your survival issues at stake in any way: are you sick, unemployed, in a dispute, at a new job, or in the process of moving? Or is something else triggering survival fears?

- How are your survival issues impacting your sense of safety?

- How safe do you feel in your relationships?

- What aspects of your life do you feel unsafe about?

- What things do others do that make you feel unsafe?

- Identify how you contribute to your partner or other people feeling unsafe.

- Do you have fears you need to heal? What are they?

---

## How Do I Create Safety?

How do we create safety for our partner and ourselves? Once we ask the right questions and figure out where we have issues that negatively impact our sense of safety (or our partner's, if we are in a relationship) we can begin to address them. We can choose to tackle fears that do not serve us. We can choose behaviors and make life decisions that create safety.

## Set an Intention

Affirmations can help us set good intentions. All action follows intention. We are much more likely to do things we intend to do. If we set an intention but are unable to follow it through, it means there is another hidden intention that is working at cross-purposes. We just haven't identified it yet.

Here is an example of a woman who set an intention but had another hidden intention that was sabotaging her. Susan wanted to get more fit. She said to herself, "I love myself no matter what shape my body is in, but I also intend to get in better shape." She was unable to stick to her diet and exercise program. This is because she had a deeper and unrecognized intention. She unconsciously said to herself, "I deserve to be comfortable. I don't want to suffer in any way." This cross-intention sabotaged her plan to get in better shape. *Note: this scenario is not true for everyone who would like to but cannot change his or her fitness habits.*

We can sabotage our relationship or ourselves when we have a hidden underlying belief that things should be easier than they are. That underlying belief prevents us from sticking through difficult times. Another underlying belief that can sabotage our intention to have a good relationship is the belief that we have to make it

okay for the other person, *even at our own expense.* This is akin to low self-esteem, and this belief will prevent our intention from fully manifesting.

Affirmations you could use in your relationship around creating safety might be:

- I love you enough to want you to feel safe with me.

- I love you enough to be on your team.

- I love you enough to listen to your feelings.

- I love us enough to make our relationship safe.


Some affirmations you can use for yourself could be:

- I love myself enough to not put up with bad behavior.

- I love myself enough to take care of myself.

- I love myself enough to listen to my intuition.

- I love myself enough to honor my need for safety.

One affirmation I've used over the years to help me feel safer has been, "Let go and let god." I learned this slogan when I attended Al-Anon many years ago. This affirmation allowed me to trust that I didn't have to do everything, and it wasn't all up to me. In this case, I am using the word "god" as an idea of a higher order and system of things, rather than as a specific being who is looking over me individually.

I "got" this affirmation when I was living in New York City and waiting for the subway. I was late. I was stressed and anxious. As I waited and waited, I realized that no amount of stressing was going to make the train come any quicker. The train would arrive when it arrived. If I was late, then I was late. I was able to release the schedule of the train, and the subsequent timetable that I had imposed on something outside of myself. While this is an example about my need to be in control, it also applied to my relationship with others. As long as I tried to manage everything, my energy was caught up in controlling. And in alignment with the principle of manifestation, I drew to myself people who were out of control.

Look at your conscious intentions and affirmations. Do you believe them? Regarding your intentions for safety, do you want them badly enough to root out whatever may be in the way? If what you want is not manifesting, then you will need to dig deeper to find what is lurking in your belief system that is stopping it. If we have areas of insecurity that impact our sense of safety or our ability to survive, we can choose to get help if needed. We can choose new responses. We can learn to deal with what is actually occurring, not a scenario that is more about a fear or a conditioned response from our past.

All of us have ghosts from our past that interfere with our ability to meet our needs. But those of us who choose to dig deep and transform these old beliefs into better ones make the most progress. This is part of choosing to be the best you can be and is part of becoming relationship-ready. Stepping into a sense of safety is a wonderful feeling. It is part of the path of manifestation. It is part of the path of magic.

## Start a New Habit

So far, I've asked what it is in your life and relationship that makes you feel unsafe. If you have answers to those questions, I encourage you to take this information and write it in your notebook in your own way. Identify where these fears come from and what you imagine may happen. What is the worst thing that could happen? Afterwards, decide what you would do about it. Even if we aren't crazy about the option, knowing what we would do in our worst-case scenario often makes us feel safer because we have a plan.

You might want to use your non-dominant hand to do this writing. The awkwardness of doing this can connect us with a vulnerable or child-like part of ourselves. With your non-dominant hand, take a pen or pencil and answer that question of what your worst-case scenario would be. Let yourself feel like a child. See what comes out.

Then take your dominant hand and "write back" to yourself about how you could handle this situation. This lets the more adult self come out and is a way of nurturing the part of you that is scared.

Wendy was afraid of standing up for herself with her boyfriend. As she wrote her feelings down with her left hand, she felt her emotions rise to the surface. She became aware that this would be scary for her and that she was afraid she would be dumped or rejected or make her partner angry. When she began to respond with her right hand, she was able to find a stronger part of herself that said, "You will be okay no matter what. I am glad when you are able to be yourself." This helped Wendy feel a little safer and made her more willing to tackle this fear.

## Ingredient One: Safety

Forming a habit or learning any new way of being takes practice and time. That is why any spiritual practice takes years before one is a master. Be patient with yourself. Set the intention to create safety for yourself or your relationship. Know that as you set your intention and begin the steps, you can change your world. Remember, a journey from one place to another takes intention, effort, and time.

# Chapter 9

## Ingredient Two: Accountability

**I am accountable to others and myself.**

---

Accountability is a big word. It stretches across the fabric of who we are and how we impact others and our world. Accountability means we are willing to look at ourselves and take responsibility for our actions. It means that we do what we say and say what we mean. It's being able to say, "I'm sorry I hurt you. How can I fix it?" Accountability makes us trustworthy.

In *The Invention of Wings* by Sue Monk Kidd, a character who is dying (I don't want to give it away to those of you who haven't

yet read this fabulous book) acknowledged some wrongs he had committed in his life. He acknowledged he defended slavery and owned slaves because his prosperity and way of life depended on it, even though he knew it was morally wrong. He acknowledged his actions came out of greed and complacency. He did not, however, rectify the situation he engendered; he did not free his slaves. His acknowledgment is a step in the direction of accountability and responsibility, yet it is just that—a step.

Imagine that you chose to tell somebody important to you that what they did was upsetting to you and made you feel as if you weren't important to them, and they responded saying, "I am so sorry. I didn't realize that would hurt you. You are important to me, and I don't want to hurt you. I won't do that again." That response would allow you to trust them and feel good about them and about yourself because they were holding themselves accountable to their actions and being responsive to your feelings.

When we are accountable, we do not push our imperfections or mistakes away. As we come to see them, we allow them to guide us to make changes to address our issues. As we take responsibility for ourselves, we increase the level of safety in our relationships. We become trustworthy and a better partner. We become somebody another person would want to be close to.

## Not Accountable

What does a relationship look like when you don't take responsibility for your choices, or if your partner or friend doesn't?

## Ingredient Two: Accountability

It can be like a relationship with a small child who broke a rule but insisted they didn't. We've all seen this scenario: "Mommy, Jamie hit me." "You hit me first." "No I didn't." Obviously somebody isn't telling the truth. While this may be normal behavior for 4-year-olds, it isn't going to work in an adult relationship.

Examples of a lack of accountability are everywhere, and we see them in the news frequently. Remember Bernie Madoff, nicknamed The Lord of Lies, who defrauded thousands of investors of billions of dollars? There are countless incidents of a lack of accountability and the hurt it causes others. It is pretty obvious in these kinds of scenarios. But this happens in more subtle ways, too, in our relationships with people we trust. Sometimes we are the ones not being accountable to others and ourselves. Sometimes others are not being accountable to us.

I once helped a dear friend get an apartment by signing a lease for her during a time when she was sober and needed help. (This was a big co-dependent mistake on my part. I wasn't letting her be accountable for the mess she had gotten herself into.) She began drinking again, and her alcoholic behavior flared up. She got into a tiff with the landlady and acted in a very disrespectful manner. When I told her that I was upset with her behavior, she became angry with me. She wasn't willing to be accountable for how she had behaved and or acknowledge that it was my name on the lease, not hers. When I signed that lease, I was agreeing to follow the terms of that lease, as well as to behave in a mature and respectful manner. Although there was the magic of love in our friendship, that magic could not

survive without the ingredient of accountability. Her unwillingness to be accountable ended our friendship.

I need to know that people will do what they say and say what they mean—myself included. Otherwise, I feel like I'm in quicksand, getting sucked down into some sticky mess. I wouldn't be able to live with myself if I didn't honor my word. Our words are powerful. They define who we are.

When we are with someone who is not accountable, we may feel angry, frustrated, unsafe, or as if we are losing our minds. It can be confusing when somebody isn't telling us the truth, won't own up to what they did or didn't do, or is out and out lying to us.

## How Do You Avoid Accountability?

One of the main roadblocks to accountability is a deep and often hidden sense of shame. Nobody likes to feel as if they are doing something wrong or that they messed up. Shame makes us want to hide our faults and pretend we don't have any. While guilt causes us to temporarily feel bad for messing up, shame tells us we are dirty, defective, or somehow intrinsically not okay. In other words, our sense of "yuckiness" does not seem fixable.

When we have underlying shame, we may be unwilling to take responsibility for our actions. We may instead shift the blame to someone else. For example, a person getting divorced may move into rage at their partner and blame them, rather than experiencing the shame of feeling like a failure in that relationship. Shame makes it very difficult to show our weaknesses or take responsibility for our mistakes because it means we have to face our feelings of being defective.

Another way we avoid accountability is when we want something more than we want a relationship. This often happens with addictions. The need to use the substance or enact the behavior overrides almost everything, including the desire to be fully relational. Often people hide when they want something that they could not get if they were honest with themselves or others.

Common ways we do not take responsibility for our needs or ourselves or are not accountable for our behavior include:

- Controlling or manipulating others, which includes needing things to be our way.

- Blaming others.

- Using others for our benefit at their expense, including sexually.

- Not owning up to our behavior or our part of a fight.

- Addiction.

- Hiding from ourselves—not going after what we really want or not allowing ourselves to experience our dreams and desires.

- Putting up with bad behavior—abdicating our wants for the sake of peace.

These are hard things to cop to. They are not pretty. I have struggled particularly with wanting to keep the peace and being afraid of asking for what I needed—mostly emotionally. I wasn't being accountable to my own needs, and this largely came from a history of not feeling that I could safely ask for what I needed.

## Do You Sacrifice Your Needs to Feel Loved?

Jane often slept with the men she dated to make them happy and because she was afraid of being rejected if she said "no"—not because she actually wanted to sleep with them. She liked sex, but she felt awful afterward if the guy didn't call her or didn't treat her like she was special to them. While this is scenario is not true for everyone, in Jane's case, she wasn't being accountable to her own need to wait until she was with someone who really liked her and felt lucky to be with her *before* she slept with them.

Jane had a wound. She was hungry to feel loved and wanted, partially because she had grown up with an absent and critical father who wasn't emotionally available, and this had caused her to feel unlovable. As an adult, rather than stand up for herself, she tried desperately to get the person she liked to adore her—even if they really didn't. She did this by trying to keep these various men happy, at great cost to her self. Because of her wound, her desperation to be loved caused her to sacrifice herself. It was very difficult for her to be accountable to her need to be with someone who was crazy about her. Although Jane was looking for a deep and authentic feeling of love, in order to manifest that, she needed to be accountable to herself and her need for someone to be there for her in a true and profound way.

Jane had a choice. She could see herself as a victim and complain that men were losers, or she could look at herself and how her choices were impacting her happiness. It wasn't men in general that were the problem, but whom she was allowing into her life (and bed) because she wasn't being responsible to her real needs.

If we make excuses for what we have done (or not done) or blame someone else, we are not taking responsibility for our actions. We are not being accountable. On the other hand, taking responsibility for our own actions means we are willing to honestly look at ourselves. It means we are grown up, and it is a big piece of being relationship-ready.

## How Accountable Are You?

It is important to identify where you struggle with your own accountability and also where you allow others to not be accountable to you. You absolutely need this ingredient to have a fabulous life and relationship. You might get *things* you want like Bernie Madoff did, but you won't get what you really desire without it. Grab your notebook and write about your sense of responsibility and accountability. You can use the following questions as a guide.

Or if you prefer, skip the following questions. Instead, close your eyes and think about accountability. Imagine being in a completely accountable relationship. Or think about a situation where you or

someone else wasn't accountable. You might get an image or a feeling. Write about whatever comes up for you.

---

- What parts of your life do you tend to blame on something or someone else?

- Are you accountable for your actions, or do you use your feelings of anger or disappointment to justify bad behavior?

- If your partner says yelling is hard for him or her, are you actively trying to find another way to communicate? Or do you make excuses for your actions?

- Do you tell your partner or someone else they should not feel the way that they do, or can you accept how he or she feels?

- Do you honor your needs? What are they?

- Do you take too much responsibility and let others off the hook? How? Be specific.

- Do you do what you say or make promises you cannot keep?

- Where are you not accountable to yourself?

---

## Look Hard at Yourself

To build this muscle of accountability, you will have to use it. In twelve-step terminology, people are asked to "take a searching and fearless inventory" of themselves. To help you with accountability:

- Take responsibility for your emotions, your desires, your behavior, and your actions. For example, if you were angry at your partner, and you put them down because you felt frustrated, you would need not only to apologize, but also to let your partner know that your behavior was not okay and that you are going to do whatever it takes to overcome this way of dealing with your frustration.

- Accept that what you do with your feelings, desires, behavior, and actions is a choice.

- Do not take responsibility for other people's failures or bad behavior. Let them be accountable for themselves.

Try saying this affirmation to yourself: "I do not have to be perfect. I only need to be accountable to others and myself." Notice what comes up for you when you say this to yourself.

Being accountable will make you look hard at yourself. This often isn't easy. The parts of you that don't want to be accountable may stand up and tell you that you don't have to. They may say, "It's not your fault. You don't have to change." Don't listen to them. They will keep you a smaller person than you have the potential to be.

## Choosing to Change

Many years ago, I learned about accountability in a big way when I got into a particularly difficult and life-changing relationship with a man who had alcohol and drug problems. I had fallen head-over-heels in love. He gave me a lot of attention. We had great sex. We had fun. Until things started getting weird, and I realized he had a serious problem. I remember sitting in the emergency room with him in the middle of the night. He had been in a bad neighborhood buying drugs and had been mugged. He was hit in the face with a metal pipe, and his jaw was broken.

After a number of unacceptable events, I realized I had a problem. I wasn't being accountable to my needs or myself. My life had started to unravel as I was more focused on him and what he was doing than on me. (This often happens in relationships where one partner is out of control or lying.) That is when I first said to myself, "I have a problem. I need to get help for me." And I did.

## Know Yourself Better

Pick an area where you haven't been accountable to yourself—where you let yourself down or don't stand up for yourself. Write about it. Decide what you can do differently to begin to change this way of relating to yourself.

Pick an area where you haven't been accountable to someone else—where you let them down in some way, lied, manipulated or blamed them for something. Find a way to begin to change this pattern. You may need to apologize. You may need to re-evaluate how you view this person and why you blame them. Write about this, too.

Give yourself a chance to get to know yourself better. There is no shame here, only a chance to see yourself more fully and to step into a more adult position. Once you have a clearer vision of where you struggle with accountability and how you want to change, ask yourself if you are ready to step forward into greater self-responsibility.

Remember to take baby steps. Writing is a good first step. Any action at all is better than having big ideas you do not carry through. Progress, not perfection, is your goal. All changes take time and perseverance, especially big changes in how you relate to others, yourself, and your world. But these changes are essential. They determine the world we all share.

If you want to read more on accountability, go to my blog post, *"Accountability and Character." [www.jenniferlehrmft. com/?p=598]*

# Chapter 10

## Ingredient Three: Empowerment

**I am empowered. I respect myself. I respect my partner.**

---

When I think of empowerment, the image I get is of a person radiating, like the sun radiates light, heat, and energy. Our sense of self-respect exudes outward. We are confident. We value ourselves. We do not compromise ourselves to be with somebody else. We also do not overstep our power and use it against another.

Imagine being in a relationship with someone who respects you and believes you are precious and amazing. You find your partner precious and amazing as well. Your relationship is based on mutual respect. You listen to, honor, and value each other. You treat each

other well, no matter how upset you might get, and if you can't, you decide to heal whatever is standing in the way. You do this because you know how painful it is to be mistreated. You do this because how you use your power is important to you.

## The Shadow Side of Empowerment

We live in a world where the abuse of power occurs constantly. Indentured servants and slavery still exists—what could be a greater abuse of power than that? Power is often abused in much more subtle ways. For example, when you sign up for a "free promo" and it turns into a paid subscription that you cannot easily get out of (this happened to my husband and me with our cable provider), this is a violation of power because it is purposeful entrapment.

I experienced an abuse of power in my family growing up. Because my father was prone to violent rages, the power balance in my family was way off. He abused his power by threatening and scaring us. I learned that anger and being powerful was negative. I watched how my father hurt all of us. When we don't have a good image of healthy empowerment, we tend to emulate one of the role models we have. In my case, the choice was either to be a bully or to please the power bearer in order to survive. I chose what seemed to be the more loving choice—pleasing the power bearer. But this position left me without a real backbone. I was terrified of confrontation. I didn't know that healthy anger was okay. I was overly concerned that the other person might become upset. I had a tendency to "please" others in order to keep them happy and myself safe. I didn't know how to say no. In short, it left me crippled in the ability to stand up for myself.

In order to become empowered, I've had to learn to stand up for myself. This process has not been easy. I had a lot of work to do in order to claim my right to be angry and my right to take a stand regardless of how the other person feels.

Now when I struggle in the area of standing up for myself, I take a good, hard look at what is going on. What have I gotten caught in? What do I need to let go of? What am I afraid of?

I also choose not to be close with people who aren't in balance with their power. I don't have the time or energy to navigate through an adult relationship where the other person isn't able to stand on their own two feet or isn't respectful of others or me. I don't want to be stuck protecting others (or myself) from them or, conversely, trying to get them to see that they are not victims.

## The Ugly Duckling

How do we find our empowerment? How do we see our beauty and value? How do we find our self-esteem?

Let us look at the story of *The Ugly Duckling*—a fairy tale originally written by Hans Christian Andersen. It starts with the amazing event of birth. The eggs have hatched, and the little ducklings are delighting in their new world outside of the confines of the shell. But one egg hadn't yet hatched. When it finally does, that little duckling isn't like the others. He is large and gangly—perhaps misshapen from being

in the egg too long according to the mother duck. Because of his appearance, the other ducks and chickens as well as the people he encounters persecute him. Wherever he goes, he is misunderstood, mistreated and belittled.

One day he sees three swans. He cannot believe how beautiful they are. He looks at them with great longing. Somehow they make his heart happy. Although they fly off, he remembers how seeing them has made him feel. He tries to hold that feeling close to him. The fall turns into cold and winter arrives. The Ugly Duckling endures more misadventures and persecution.

One beautiful spring morning he sees the swans again. He wants to be with them even if they are to kill him. When he approaches them, they swim towards him, and he is sure he is to be killed. As he bows his head down, from the surface of the water, his reflection—a graceful and beautiful swan looks up at him. I suspect he cannot believe the beauty he sees. The other swans welcome him with love and acceptance and the local children yell their delight at his beauty.

The Ugly Duckling feels ashamed at first. Then he raises his head and cries with joy, "I never dreamed of such happiness as this while I was an ugly duckling."

He no longer sees himself as less than. Nor does he see himself as better than. Instead, he comes to embody his own being-ness. He comes to believe that he is beautiful, worthy and has value. In accepting himself, he comes home to his true identity and also finds the support of others.

## Ingredient Three: Empowerment

Initially, because he was in a sense born 'out of place,' he wasn't able to see whom he was. That happened later, after many trials and tribulations. Although he didn't consciously step into his power, he was growing and changing. At some point when the opportunity opened, he decided he would rather face death and meet the beautiful swans (himself) than live alienated from his true identity.

## Do You Like Yourself?

If we do not have a healthy sense of self-respect and self-esteem, how will we be able to treat our partner or ourselves appropriately? Imagine your life if you didn't like yourself or were ashamed of yourself. Who would you pick as a partner? What would you put up with?

That was how I felt earlier in my life. I felt I was too skinny, not pretty enough, not smart enough, not able to fit in, and simply not okay. I had a lot of history around this way of seeing myself, and it contributed to my getting off to a difficult start in my relationships.

This is not the case anymore. I consider myself empowered and am certainly on the path of becoming more empowered. I've worked long and hard for this ability, and it is something I love about myself. I respect myself. I have good self-esteem. I can say "no" if I need to. I can let things go when I choose. I am my own authority, and that feels great. I also don't push other people around. I see myself with more accuracy and appreciate myself. I have a lot of good qualities, and I am a fantastic partner—just ask my husband.

## Domestic Violence

Most of us never expect to be a victim of domestic violence. Yet this abuse of power happens every day—frequently. Often in these cases, the abused partner feels trapped and is unable to escape, or they are seduced by the "good" times, thinking the abuse has stopped permanently. Both members of the couple caught in the trap of domestic violence invariably have underlying shame, anger, and self-esteem issues.

## What About Shame?

People with healthy self-esteem don't put up with bad behavior. They also don't mistreat others. Low self-esteem is the opposite of empowerment. If you don't have healthy self-esteem, you may allow yourself to be pushed around, either by a person or circumstances. You may take responsibility for others' problems or not ask for enough yourself. Or if your self-esteem is distorted, you may demand that everything be your way or not face up to how you have let others down.

These kinds of issues often originate from early shaming experiences. Perhaps we weren't treated well as a child. Perhaps we were told we were bad. Unfortunately, children would rather believe *they* are bad than believe that the world is unfair or that they have bad parents. It is easier to blame ourselves than face a world that feels unfair. When we believe we are bad, we feel shame about ourselves. We feel defective.

## Ingredient Three: Empowerment

A person's sense of shame can manifest as someone who is judgmental (pushing shame onto someone else) or as someone who feels worthless (internalizing shame). Most bullies are not empowered and, deep down, do not feel good about themselves. They take their sense of shame and defectiveness or even feelings of emotional hunger and push that onto someone else so they don't have to feel it. I call this "passing the hot potato." Often there are other issues of fear and needing to control entwined with this.

If you have the problem of mistreating or pushing others around, then you will have to dig down to the wound driving your behavior so you can heal and change how you feel about yourself, as well as change your behavior towards others. If you have internalized shame, it means you have work to do around finding your sense of value and worthiness.

Having self-esteem means learning not to accept someone else's judgment of you. Ultimately, it means you can have compassion for them and yourself while not believing the message they are trying to give to you. You need healthy self-esteem to be empowered. If you don't have good self-esteem, no other person (partner, friend, or relative) is going to be able to give it to you.

When we are in balance with our power, we use it appropriately. We do not need to have others "do it our way" or manipulate or push someone else around. We ask for what we need without being pushy. We respect others, including our partner. People want to know us and value us because of our healthy sense of empowerment and relationship with ourselves.

## Telltale Signs of Undervaluing Ourselves

Here are some signs that we undervalue ourselves.

- We are afraid to ask for what we want.

- We do not believe we deserve to be treated well.

- We put ourselves down.

- We feel resentment instead of standing up for ourselves.

- We don't know how to say no.

## Telltale Signs of Overvaluing Ourselves

Signs that we have issues of overvaluing our needs instead of being able to function in a two-person relationship include:

- We are abusive, put the others down, or feel judgmental.

- We have to have things our way or expect to be catered to.

- We have difficulty respecting other people's differences.

- We think we are better than others.

People who don't feel like they deserve, generally don't get. People who feel as if they are more entitled than others often hurt others and injure their relationships. Finding your empowered self means healing the parts of yourself that feel shame or not good enough.

Being in correct alignment with your power will allow you to be in an equal partnership. If one person is the king or queen and the other is the servant, then you are not in an equal, respectful relationship, and neither person is in balance with their power.

## Take a Look

It is time to dig deep again and take a clear and honest look at yourself in the area of empowerment, which includes respect of self and others. Your future self needs you to become a fully empowered and relational being. Grab your notebook and write about your self-esteem and sense of self-empowerment. You can use the following questions as a guide.

Or if you prefer, skip the following questions. Instead, close your eyes and think about empowerment. Imagine feeling completely empowered. You might get an image or a feeling. Write about whatever comes up for you.

---

- In what ways do you like or feel good about yourself?
- Do you feel better than others? In what ways?
- Do you ever overpower others? How?
- Do you avoid being powerful? How?
- Do you get caught in resentment instead of action?
- Can you accept that your partner isn't going to agree with everything and may make choices you dislike?

---

## Do You Push or Get Pushed?

You know your relationship tendencies. Do you tend to push others to get your way, or do you tend to get pushed around or hide? Or maybe this is not a problem for you.

If you accept somebody else's or your own rejection of who you are by not showing yourself or hiding, it may be time to confront this. Your thoughts and feelings deserve to be spoken, even if they are not always popular. Dialog implies exposure and risk, but also allows a fuller relationship with others. Practice taking care of yourself, even when the other person wants something different than you or sees things differently. Though if you are with a person who is inflexible or just cannot understand your position, having a distant relationship may be the only way to go.

If you tend to push people around, start looking at your feelings about not getting what you think you want. Don't get caught in choosing to have your way over having a relationship. Remember the saying, "you can be right, or you can have a relationship." They are talking to you.

## Susan's Dream

Often, following a dream takes us down the path of becoming more empowered.

Susan had a dream. She wanted to become a photographer. She was good at her job at the bank where she worked, but it didn't fill her soul. Her parents had not supported her in believing that she could be whoever she wanted to be. She didn't have much self-confidence or a sense of her own value. Deep down, she didn't like herself. She liked it if others complimented her, but she couldn't say good things about herself. Susan's boyfriend Zack loved her dearly but hated watching her mistreat herself. It was hard for him to be with her when she was depressed. He encouraged her to spend more time taking photographs and suggested that she take a class.

Susan listened to Zack. She began to explore her creative side. Although she was very insecure about her photographs at first, she began to like them. She stopped putting herself down so much. Zack was proud of her. He started feeling better about their relationship because Susan was happier and felt better about herself. Their relationship began to improve. Eventually, Susan built a business around her photography, and Zack and Susan's life together became fuller. Zack began to see Susan as someone he could commit to long term because she liked herself and was happier. As Susan became more empowered, Zack and Susan became closer.

Learning to be empowered is a process. It doesn't happen overnight. It is a muscle that must be built. If this is an area you would like to focus on, it may be helpful to read rags-to-riches stories of empowered people—people like Oprah, Wayne Dyer, and others. These are people who said to themselves, "I deserve to follow my dreams. I deserve to be treated well. I deserve a partner who adores me."

Some helpful affirmations for empowerment are:

- I honor myself enough to follow my dreams.

- I value myself and see myself as worthy.

- I love myself enough not to tolerate bad behavior.

- I value others, so I am kind to them and treat them with respect.

- I don't need things to always go my way.

- I stand up for myself.

Can you say those things to yourself? Do you believe them? Sometimes we simply have to act as if we are already there. This means we decide what the appropriate behavior or action is, and we do it, even if it is difficult. This is an area where we often need support, like a twelve-step group or therapy. Or even stepping out into the world to accomplish something can be helpful in increasing self-esteem and a sense of empowerment.

## What Do You Tell Yourself?

Listen to your self-talk. What do you tell yourself? Are you critical? Often when we were younger, if somebody treated us without respect or was critical to us, we internalized that critical voice. We grew up, but we sometimes continue to experience life through that negative filter. Do you have a little voice inside that tells you that you are not good enough, or you have to try harder? You may believe logically that you are fine but often may feel differently or have a voice inside that tells you otherwise.

## Ingredient Three: Empowerment

Write down the things you say to yourself. Write down what you would like to say to yourself. It should be what you would say to someone you loved and adored. You don't mistreat someone you love—including yourself.

Another exercise is to find the younger parts of you. This is called "inner-child work," and there are a number of books that can help you with this. Or you can try to imagine the child within you and give him or her a voice. Find out how your inner child feels. When we have disparaging inner voices that tell us we are not okay, we probably have an inner child that feels abandoned and hurt. We may have to "re-parent" ourselves by finding the loving part of ourselves and talk to and care for our "smaller" or more hurt parts. Treat that part of yourself, as you would treat a small child you adore. As we give ourselves the supportive experience we did not have the first time around, we can begin to strengthen our self-esteem.

### The Doubter

Susan, the photographer in the preceding story, had a part of her that said, "You won't find your dream." She named this part "The Doubter." She had to address this part of herself. She was able to say to The Doubter, "I know you are afraid I will get hurt, and you want me to stay small to protect me, but I am willing to step out into the world and try to make my dream a reality." And she did!

Try to find the emotional part of you that feels unworthy or mistreated or stops you from finding your power and following your dreams. It helps to name these parts. Write them down. What would

you like to say to each of them? See if you can figure out how each part is trying to help you first. (Our inner parts often are trying to help us in misguided ways.) Then write to it. Explain how you appreciate the intention of this part, but tell it how you see things and what you want to do. Ask it to trust you.

If you would like to read more about the connection between feeling like a victim and being empowered, go to my blog post, *"Anatomy of an Emotional Victim: Changing Victim Consciousness to Self-Empowerment." [www.jenniferlehrmft. com/?p=257]*

# Chapter 11

## Ingredient Four: Compassion

**I am able to give and receive love freely.**

Love *cares*. We know when we are loved and when we are not. We know when we are cared about and when we are not. Like Mother Teresa's love or the pure love you pour upon a newborn infant, we are able to radiate love. This love transforms the unseen or undeveloped because it recognizes intrinsic value and beauty. This love heals.

Love is expressed; it is our actions. (Are our actions loving?) It is our attitude. (Are we respectful? Do we have empathy, compassion, gratitude, and appreciation?) And it is a feeling.

Allow love to be a guiding principle in your life and your relationships.

## Can You Love a Partner Like a Cat?

When I told my husband I was writing a little segment on whether loving your partner is like loving your cat; he laughed and said, "I hope so!" Life (and love) would be a lot easier if it was, but unfortunately it is different. Loving a person is much more difficult.

After my first husband and I had purchased a house, we decided to get a kitten. We wanted a tabby and went to the local animal shelter to find one. There was only one tabby kitten there: a tiny, gray tabby all by himself in a cage. When we took him out, he grabbed onto my husband's shirt and would not let go. He picked us, and we went with his decision. We named him Hank.

Hank was an amazing being who became my constant companion. He was the emotional support I went to on a daily basis. He even made the bed with me. I would whip the bottom sheet into the air; and as it floated down onto the mattress, Hank would race across the mattress furiously, delighting in the sheet slowly coming down over his body, clawing at the mattress in excitement. Then I would have to get him out from under the sheet so I could finish putting it on. He repeated the performance with the top sheet, except I would grab at his body encased in the sheet; and he would enthusiastically attack and roll and run. Making a bed has never been as fun before or since Hank.

## Ingredient Four: Compassion

I love my current husband a lot. I consider him to be my soul partner. But loving a person is filled with challenges. My husband challenges me to grow, though not always intentionally. Although he is usually supportive, he also does things that are difficult for me, or that I find challenging. He sometimes annoys me. I do get upset with him. We occasionally fight. I sometimes feel abandoned when he gets caught up in his own agenda. And I challenge him to grow as well. Getting through these challenges requires tenacity, patience, and the ability to communicate and choose to love even when I don't feel like being loving. This part of love is not easy.

These two kinds of love are different. Hank (who passed away in 2011) was my avatar, a deity of big proportions, and he was always emotionally present for me. And my love for Hank was completely unconditional. He didn't piss me off. He never disappointed me. He was always loving. We didn't fight. He was my emotional go-to when I was upset. He got me through a difficult marriage and an even more difficult divorce. And my compassion for him was constant.

With my husband, it is not so simple. We've done a lot of psychological work together: figuring out how we triggered each other and learning how to bridge the gap created by disappointment, hurt, and differing needs. We've learned to understand and have compassion for each other during those difficult moments that inevitably occur. Loving an adult is a more challenging kind of love than loving a pet or baby. Loving a person means we will have to stretch and grow.

## Imagine an Amazing Love

A close, loving relationship is such a wonderful feeling. It is the stuff of dreams, the feeling of being showered with love by your beloved, of being folded into a cocoon of adoration. It is knowing that no matter what, your partner feels empathy and has compassion for you - and you for him or her.

Love is not an abstract idea or a fleeting feeling, but an action. Love means you treat each other with care, even when you run into a difficulty, even when you are hurt or disappointed. Love means you feel appreciation and gratitude for your beloved; your hearts are open, and the love between you flows. Underneath any difficulties, there is an absolute love each of us needs.

Loving is similar to the feeling of falling in love, except it is more permanent because you know who your partner is, faults and all. You are able to get through challenges, conflicts, and disappointments, and you love each other anyway. Your love is no longer fragile, ready to vanish whenever a conflict emerges. Your love is solid and strong.

## We Need Love

My life would feel empty without love, not just of my husband, my family and friends, but love for the sky, for the trees, for my dogs, for humanity, for the animal kingdom, for myself—for all the beings of this earth. For me, it is the experience of love, both loving and being loved that makes life worthwhile despite pain and difficulty. And it is the capacity to love that makes all of our lives beautiful.

## Ingredient Four: Compassion

Many of the horrible events in the world occur because of a lack of real love.

We've all been in situations where we felt anger, judgment, criticism, or even hatred coming at us. Or we just weren't seen or validated. Feeling unloved is one of the worst feelings there is.

We need to know that our partner can see our struggles with empathy and compassion. We need to know we are precious to them and that they hold us in their heart and value us. We need to know we are truly loved.

We have enormous power in how we treat others and whether they feel our love or not. Through the power of our love, we can transform each other's lives.

## How Loving Are You?

Love is easy when we are "in love," and everything feels wonderful. But life and relationships entail more than easy or superficial interactions. Challenges to our ability to love are frequent and common. Having an open heart is often difficult when we feel hurt or disappointed, which sooner or later, is bound to occur in every relationship. Nobody is perfect. We all make mistakes, have character flaws, and have areas where our hearts are closed. Our partner may be too anxious, too tidy, too selfish, too generous, too demanding, or something else. On top of this, it is common to have wounds around loving, places where we weren't loved perfectly in the past that are activated easily.

Whatever it is, being loving when these "flaws" are triggered can take us to the mat. It is easy to either "close up" and push love away, or to "get intense," which also pushes love away. While we have these actions because we are hurt or afraid, beneath it all, we want connection and love.

One particularly difficult disruption in a relationship is when our "wounds collide." This means both partners simultaneously hit each other's deepest wound. With both people regressed or shut down, keeping an open heart is generally impossible. Instead, we can learn how to talk about each of our wounds and gain enough understanding of each other (and ourselves) so we can eventually heal this wound and get through these situations more easily.

When I look back on some of the fights I've had in past relationships and with my husband, I can remember the big ones: the times my partner completely did not see something I needed, or judged me instead of having empathy and compassion for my need or fear. The pain of not feeling cared for regarding a very specific need is brutal. It takes me to a place where I feel unloved, abandoned, and alone.

When I feel that way, I become self-protective and tend to close up and pull away. I've learned how to not pull away, but instead to be emotionally present and available even when I am upset. Because I can see that my partner is hurting too, I am now able to keep my heart open. This helps my relationship tremendously. When both people are able to do this, conflicts are resolved more easily, more quickly, and with less pain.

Part of maintaining an open heart is understanding that whatever weakness our partner has or we have is part of our path of learning and growing. We can have empathy and compassion for our partner's struggles if we see how these things *hurt* them too—not just us.

(It may look like a selfish person is not being hurt, but being caught in the experience of selfishness or meanness results in that person's life being compressed and truncated. It is not the kind of experience a vibrantly loving person would want to have. I sure don't want to feel those yucky feelings you get when you aren't being your best self or living your best life.)

## David and Becca's Story

Here is a story about David and Becca's struggle. David has a lot of good qualities. He is good looking, upbeat, and fun to talk to. He makes a good income, and he likes nice things. But he sees the world as if *it owes him*. And he isn't generous. David is married to Becca. She was happy with the lifestyle David provided them and loved her husband's intellect and charm. But when Becca's dad, Bert, got sick and needed care he could not afford, David was unwilling to help. Becca was beside herself. She couldn't believe her husband would be so selfish—not just to her father, but also to her feelings of needing to help her father. Becca became angry and combative. David felt like nothing he did was right. He felt unloved and confused.

Becca hated how she was feeling and what was happening to her marriage. She did a lot of soul searching and came to understand more of David's character. She saw that David had been spoiled as a child so he expected to be given to. He also had a father who didn't

take care of him emotionally. This created a wound in David and left him resenting his father. The last thing David wanted to do was to take care of someone else. "Each man to himself" was his motto. It wasn't a very open-hearted position.

This aspect of her husband was very difficult for Becca, and she struggled to keep her heart open toward him. She kept reminding herself that David had learning and growing to do in the area of generosity. This was his own limitation, and it hurt him more than anyone else. She had to remember he had his own wounds and that he had many loveable qualities as well. Eventually, Becca was able to get David to understand her feelings and how important helping her father was to her. They worked out a compromise, and their marriage improved.

For a different and more detailed example of wounds colliding, read my blog post *"When Wounds Collide." [www.jenniferlehrmft. com/?p=13]*

Learning to love through our wounds and the challenges of our differences is a tall order. It takes time. But it is worthwhile because it is the bridge across our differences that allows our love to flow.

## Look at Your Heart

Do you know when your heart is open with empathy and compassion and when it closes? Your ability to have empathy and compassion is a wonderful quality that goes a long way in a relationship. Often our wounds make it difficult to keep an open heart. Grab your notebook and write about your ability to have compassion and empathy—especially when you feel challenged. You can use the following questions as a guide.

Or if you prefer, skip the following questions. Instead, close your eyes and think about having a completely open heart. Imagine that sense of a fully open heart. You might get an image or a feeling. Write about whatever comes up for you.

———————————————

- What causes you to feel disappointed in or to blame or judge others?

- When do you feel resentful?

- Under what circumstances do you judge or blame yourself?

- When are you disappointed in yourself?

- Who most often triggers you to feel blame, resentment, judgment, or disappointment? Why? What need of yours is not being met?

- What do you wish could be different about these situations?

- Are you able to have empathy and feel compassion when your partner opens up to you in a vulnerable way?

- When is your heart fully open?

———————————————

## Your Wounds Can Shut Your Heart

As you look at what causes you to feel these more negative emotions, notice the need that isn't being met or a past wound from a need that wasn't met. When we have a wound, our upset feelings block our ability to feel compassion, empathy, and love. Usually, until our upset feelings are calmed down, we can't be loving. Learning about our wounds, uncovering them, and attending to them is the best way to begin to heal our ability to love.

Sally struggled with her feelings of love towards her brother Tom at times. She found Tom to be self-centered and pushy. As she looked at her feelings of judgment and resentment, she realized that she felt like she was invisible to Tom. She felt unloved by Tom. She came to realize Tom had his own wounds and damage that made him unable to acknowledge her.

As Sally was able to see Tom's wounds and let go of her need for Tom to be there for her, she began to feel more loving towards him. She realized she loved Tom, even though she wanted more from their relationship. She came to accept that she could not have the close kind of relationship she wanted with Tom, and she could not spend a great deal of time with him. It was too painful. She came to accept Tom for who he was but filled her life with other, more nourishing people so that she didn't have to rely on Tom for the support she needed.

When somebody isn't meeting our needs, learning to understand his or her challenges or struggles can help us gain empathy and compassion for them. If you can put yourself in their shoes, then whatever is occurring makes more sense. Having compassion for yourself when your needs aren't being met is also important.

Part of loving is accepting others and their limitations. Another part of loving is learning to bridge disconnections by communicating with vulnerability. You'll learn more about that in the next chapter.

## Letting Go of Judgment

Julie's boyfriend Zack often would hum to himself when he felt tense. It bugged Julie because it made her feel as if he was daydreaming and not paying attention. It made her see him as weak and weird. As Julie got to know Zack better, she learned that as a child he had witnessed a lot of fighting between his parents. Distressed by the yelling and slamming doors, Zack had tried to calm himself down and pretend things were okay by humming to himself. Humming was an old (and harmless) habit left over from his childhood.

Julie also realized that it was very important to her to feel as if her partner was paying attention to her. She had wounds about not being listened to. Julie was able to stop judging Zack and have more compassion for him and his difficulty with conflict. She was also able to help him talk more about his feelings of angst, instead of trying to hum them away. Because Julie was interested in being there for her boyfriend and wanted to understand him, she was able to accept him more fully, as well as help him understand his behavior.

To help your partner become more aware of a wound that is impacting his or her behavior, you will have to learn about your

partner's wounds and earlier childhood dynamics. Generally, you will need to talk to your partner to learn their story. This is one way we develop empathy. (Interestingly, reading literary novels helps us develop empathy because we are learning to imagine the world through another person's eyes.) We have to be interested in and accepting of their world. As we do this, we are growing a bigger heart.

## What Are Your Wounds?

You can learn more about your self-image and your worldview by looking at whom you have empathy for.

For whom do you feel empathy and compassion? How do you identify with them? For example, Marvin saw his mother struggle with taking care of the family while his father was drinking at the bar. Consequently, Marvin has a very soft spot and a lot of compassion for single mothers and women with "deadbeat" husbands.

Similarly, you can figure out where your wounds are fairly easily by looking at your triggers and what upsets you.

Where are the areas you get into conflict with others? Write down a conflict you have had. See if you can identify the deep hurt you experienced that caused a wound for you. Did you feel left out, forgotten, abandoned, not valued, or not good enough; or was it something else? Identify the wound. Find empathy for yourself around this wound.

Now pick a situation or person that causes you to feel judgmental or to experience some other unloving feelings. Write down the scenario in detail. What is the main feeling you are having? Perhaps you have a relative or friend who is pushy, and you tend to feel annoyed at or hurt by this person. Now identify the need you have that is not getting met. For example, you may be feeling as if that person is not tuned into you and you feel unseen.

Or it may be about something more loosely related to this. For example, you may judge competitive people because your mother was competitive with you, and you have a wound there. Try to make the connection between your closed heart and some kind of hurt or disappointment you have had that is related to this situation. Once you find it, have empathy for the part of you that did not get your needs met. As you heal your wound, your ability to love will increase.

You may be able to extend a sense of empathy to the "trigger" or person who is causing your heart to shut down. If not, that is okay. You will have the rest of your life to work on this.

There is nothing wrong with anger when we've been hurt or mistreated. It is healthy. But learning to see the wounds of others (and our own) and developing compassion helps us enormously — especially in getting through relationship challenges.

For an article on holding both compassion and boundaries at the same time, read my blog posting, *"What Is Compassion?" [www. jenniferlehrmft.com/?p=846]*

# Chapter 12

## Ingredient Five: Vulnerability

**I am able to communicate with and listen
supportively to vulnerability.**

---

Vulnerability means you can let yourselves connect with and be present to your deeper feelings, as well as allow them to be part of your safe and intimate relationships. You allow yourself to feel your vulnerable feelings of guilt, shame, sadness, fear, joy, or excitement. You show your feelings fully. There is nothing to hide. You become softer and less defensive.

You no longer use sarcasm, logic, criticism, judgment, bitterness, anger, or resentment to push away your deeper feelings or keep

them from being a part of your intimate relationships. You know that love is only a fantasy if you don't share your vulnerable self.

As you are vulnerable with your trusted person, and they respond to your vulnerability with empathy and compassion, the unhealed parts of each of you begin to heal.

When your partner is vulnerable with you, you feel happy that they entrust their most sensitive places to you. You want to hear your partner's deep feelings and tell them yours because you want to know each other fully.

As you come to know each other more, your relationship becomes closer and closer. Your hearts connect through your vulnerabilities. Vulnerability held with compassion is the path to greater and greater love—real love, safe love, strong love.

## The Velveteen Rabbit

I looked this one up in the dictionary because it is a bit tricky. What does vulnerability actually mean? The definition is "capable of being physically or emotionally wounded." Why would anyone want that—to have the capacity to be wounded? Why is vulnerability something we need?

If you ever read the wonderful children's book, *The Velveteen Rabbit,* by Margery Williams, you may remember these words:

**The Rabbit sighed. He thought it would be a long time before this magic called Real happened to him. He longed**

to become Real, to know what it felt like; and yet the idea of growing shabby and losing his eyes and whiskers was rather sad. He wished that he could become it without these uncomfortable things happening to him.

Rabbit is talking about vulnerability. That new and shiny stuffed animal wanted to be real. He wanted to be part of life. He knew vulnerability was the path to being real. Yet, the cost was having raggedy worn spots and losing his button eyes. Like all of us, we want a real life and real love. But having a real life and a real love entails pain and difficulty, and being open about those feelings is vulnerability.

We get hurt; we suffer disappointments, and we become old and frail: we are vulnerable. When I share my vulnerability, I am showing the real lovable me, not the polished fake and perfect version (which I never was anyway). It is the genuine human part I love. We need our vulnerability because our wounds make us real, human, and loveable. Caring for one another and being cared for comes out of knowing and understanding each other—seeing our vulnerabilities, fears, and wounds. Our imperfections are not something to be ashamed of, but an expression of our humanness and a part of our path.

## Vulnerability Is a Bridge

When we first fall in love, we love who we think our partner is— that shiny, new, perfect person who makes us feel so good. At this

stage, much of our love is based on fantasy and chemistry because we don't yet know the real person. That happens later as we run into differences and disappointments. It happens when we find out that the person we love doesn't believe in helping the homeless – and we do. It happens when our partner flirts with a cute girl in front of us. It happens when our partner won't spend a holiday with our parents because he or she doesn't like them. Those disappointments hurt. And for a relationship to survive them, they cannot be hidden in the closet or swept under the rug. They have to be bridged.

Vulnerable communication allows us to bridge the gap that lies between us. As we communicate openly and with vulnerability, we learn who this other person is, not just their thoughts and ideas, but their deepest feelings, disappointments, yearnings, and dreams. And they learn about us.

Take Kelly and Tom. Kelly says, "I felt ignored, embarrassed, and ashamed when you flirted with Susan in front of me. Can you understand how that hurt me?" Even though Tom said he didn't mean anything by it and was just having fun, he learns how that flirtation made Kelly feel. Tom has the opportunity to realize that his desire for attention causes too much pain for Kelly to be viable. Or with another couple, Diana learns that her partner Billy needs her to be part of his family on holidays, even if it is difficult. And he learns why his family is difficult for her.

We get to learn how each of us feels deep down. We learn how our actions impact each other. We learn what each of us needs. We learn to tend to our partner and care for them because we love them.

## Ingredient Five: Vulnerability

Vulnerable communication is the bridge that connects two hearts and two worlds.

## How Vulnerable Are You Able to Be?

There is so much wounding in the area of vulnerability. "An eye for an eye" is the opposite of vulnerable communication. When we are upset, we tend to move into self-protection—arguing, defending, demanding, and even explaining—so easily. Self-protection is a roadblock to openly given and unguarded love. While we all need the ability to protect ourselves, ideally, self-protection is not part of an intimate, connected love relationship.

Can you be vulnerable; or are you too scared, too angry, or too guarded? There are many reasons why a person is not able to be completely open. Oftentimes we have a wound where we didn't feel loved in the past, including times when we felt scared, ignored or criticized as children. Or we may be "on guard," if we have been let down and disappointed in the past. This causes us to be cautious about sharing our vulnerable feelings. We may hide because we fear the emotional repercussions of being transparent. Maybe it isn't safe to be forthright about what we feel or need.

Some of us haven't been taught to be vulnerable. Perhaps our parents weren't vulnerable with each other or with us. We often haven't learned to communicate with vulnerability because our parents weren't good at listening. How often did they ask about your inner world, your deep feelings, and your desires? How often did you share your insecurities or hurts with them? I know I didn't. I

remember listening to my father talking about his struggles. But for most of his life, I never shared any of mine with him. I wish I had been courageous enough to share more of myself with him in the years before he died.

We may not have learned to say, "When you come home and go straight to the computer, I feel sad and alone." Or instead of saying, "When you stayed out and didn't call, I felt hurt and abandoned," we tend to get angry and hide our hurt feelings.

These wounded parts of us can stop us from being vulnerable in a relationship. Like a cornered wild animal, we push back, showing our fangs instead of our belly. These wounds can cause us to be reactive instead of being able to show our vulnerability. They can cause us to be critical instead of creating a safe place for our partner to be vulnerable with us.

## Learning to Listen

Here is a story about learning to listen supportively to vulnerability. Nick wasn't good at understanding his feelings. He would snap at his girlfriend Karen sometimes when they were in an argument. "Stop being so emotional. I hate it when you cry." Karen, of course, would get even more upset. Nick couldn't identify what he was feeling deep down, but he knew he was annoyed by Karen's behavior. Nick and Karen's relationship hit a crisis point. They frequently fought and were thinking of ending it, so they decided to get some help.

With help, Nick came to understand why Karen's emotions upset him so much. (He was developing insight—the next ingredient.)

## Ingredient Five: Vulnerability

Nick began to see that he had feelings about her emotions. When Karen cried, Nick felt bad about himself. He felt like he could not do anything right. He felt upset that she was upset and that he couldn't keep her happy. He felt like he wasn't a good boyfriend, but he didn't let himself think these thoughts or feel these feelings. They were locked away.

Instead of experiencing his deeper vulnerable feelings, Nick got angry when Karen cried. He didn't know why. As Nick explored more of his feelings, he realized his mother would get drunk and cry when he was a child. He hated that. While he wanted to take care of his mother, he was also angry at her for not being there for him. Once he identified how Karen's crying reminded him of his mother, he could begin to see that she wasn't an out-of-control, depressed alcoholic like his mother was. And he could get in touch with his deeper vulnerable feelings of loss and not being good enough.

Nick needed to be able to connect with his vulnerable feelings so he would stop rejecting Karen's vulnerable feelings. He needed to be able to say to Karen, "I feel so horrible when you cry. It makes me doubt my ability to be a good partner. Please stop. I don't want to make you cry."

Initially, Nick hadn't let himself explore his vulnerable feelings deeply enough to realize that this was what was going on for him. Once he had, they had real conversations about each of their feelings. He stopped trying to "shut her up," and their connection improved immensely.

## Walking on Egg Shells

If you find yourself "walking on egg shells," then you probably have a fear of the consequences of communicating. Often, we don't communicate because we have learned from past experience that the price is too high. And we don't want to fight. But stuffing feelings won't work in the long run because it means there is a disconnection between us. We aren't showing all of ourselves. We aren't yet being real with our partner. We aren't revealing our missing button-eyes and the worn spots on our fur, nor being loved despite them.

If you find yourself walking on egg shells, you will have to determine if it is safe to open up more or what would make it safe to do so. As long as your partner doesn't get abusive, it is probably worthwhile to communicate. If your partner is reactive in an angry and critical way, it will be difficult to communicate with vulnerability, if at all. Vulnerability requires safety.

## A Real Conversation

Jim arrived late to pick up Judy yet again, and she was fuming. When Jim got there, she lit into him. "I can't believe you are late!" she screamed. Jim tried to explain that he had lost track of the time. "Can't you just relax? It isn't such a big deal," he said. This made Judy even madder. They got into a fight, and both had a stressful and disappointing evening. Judy and Jim knew that they had not handled things very well. They wanted to reconnect and try to understand each other better. So the next day, they shared their more vulnerable feelings with each other.

Judy: It made me feel alone and not important when you were late. My parents always were late and forgot important events in my life. Because I love you, I need you to consider my feelings.

Jim: I'm sorry. I didn't mean to make you feel that way. I just get caught up in what I'm doing all the time. I think I'm late for everything.

Judy: Do you think you could set an alarm or make an extra effort to show up on time? It would really be nice for me, and it would make me feel like you care.

Jim: I will set myself a reminder on my phone next time. I feel bad that I upset you and let you down. I want you to feel you can count on me. You are important to me.

Can you hear the caring in this conversation? Judy was letting Jim know how he impacted her. She wasn't accusing or attacking him during this conversation. And Jim was letting Judy know that he cared and was willing to look at his behavior and make a change.

Vulnerability is the glue of love. Learn to feel it. Learn to share it. It is an irreplaceable element of true closeness and intimacy.

## Vulner-Ability

Have you developed your ability to be vulnerable? Can you hear the vulnerable feelings of others? Can you share your own

vulnerability? Are you aware of your deeper vulnerable feelings? Without this ability, your relationship will be less alive, juicy and intimate. Grab your notebook and write about your ability to be vulnerable. You can use the following questions as a guide.

Or if you prefer, skip the following questions. Instead, close your eyes and think about your vulnerability. Imagine sharing your vulnerability with someone else. You might get an image or a feeling. Write about whatever comes up for you.

---

- Can you identify your deeper vulnerable feelings? (Sometimes this is where we need to start.)

- Which of your vulnerable feelings (fear, guilt, shame, hurt, sadness) are you comfortable with? Uncomfortable with?

- Are you willing to share your vulnerable feelings, experiences, and needs with people you are close to? If not, what stops you? Are you afraid? Not interested?

- Are you willing to listen to the vulnerable feelings of those you are close to?

- Does listening to someone else's vulnerable feelings make you feel uncomfortable? Why?

- Are you able to have vulnerable discussions when conflicts occur?

## Awareness

By noticing your relationship with vulnerability, you will learn more about yourself and increase your ability to become more vulnerable.

- Notice when you are able to *experience* your vulnerable feelings and when you are not.

- Notice when you are able to *express* your vulnerable feelings and when you are not.

- Notice when you are able to *listen* to your partner's or another important person's vulnerable feelings and when you are not.

It is important to know what shuts down your ability to share with vulnerability or to listen to the vulnerable feelings of others. Often we shut down our hearts (and vulnerability) when we feel threatened in some way. I know that I tend to hold back on being vulnerable when I feel scared.

## Why Not?

When we are not able to be vulnerable, there is a reason. These reasons could include:

- The past is causing me to be defensive or self-protective.

- My current relationship is unsafe emotionally.

- My partner and I have not yet learned how to connect with and or express our vulnerable feelings and support each other in doing so.

Which of the above are true for you?

## Helpful Affirmations

Learning to be vulnerable can be new and scary, especially if you grew up in a household without this kind of communication. Affirmations can help support us in being vulnerable.

- My vulnerable feelings are a valuable part of our relationship and myself. I choose to honor them and express them.

- I choose to listen to my partner's vulnerable feelings.

- I want to be close to my partner (or friend). I am willing to share in a vulnerable way.

## Talking About Our Past

Here is an example of how communicating and listening with vulnerability about our past history can help a relationship.

Bobby loved watching football. He'd grab a beer and hunker down on the couch for hours. His girlfriend Tia liked to do things with Bobby on the weekends during games. She didn't like sports. She didn't like her boyfriend on the couch all day drinking beer. This became an ongoing conflict for them. They didn't see eye to eye, and they didn't know how to talk about it. They fought. It was one of the areas where they ran into conflict frequently.

Eventually, they got some help with communicating. Tia was able to explain how when Bobby spent all day on the couch, it reminded her of her dad when he was unemployed and depressed. And it made her feel unimportant and unloved—exactly the same feelings her father triggered in her. She was able to say, "I feel so abandoned when you don't want to spend time with me."

Bobby was able to talk about how he felt when she nagged him; it reminded him of his mother who always needed him to talk to her and didn't really let him do his own thing. He had felt as if he couldn't keep his mother happy and that she was a burden. (And she *was* a burden because she was looking for emotional support from her son instead of her husband or friends.) He was able to say; "I feel like I can't keep you happy, and then I feel like a failure. I want you to be happy, but I am just not good at this." Bobby was able to explain to her that he was wanted to spend time with her but that he also loved watching football, and it was a part of his life.

They both came to understand each other better as they communicated their vulnerable feelings connected to their pasts. Once they understood each other and didn't feel they were going to lose something that was valuable to each of them (connection for Tia and feeling "good enough" for Bobby), everything got easier. Tia began to spend more time by herself or go out with a friend when Bobby was "glued" to the set. And Bobby was able to "unglue" himself from the games more often and do more with his girlfriend. As they learned more about their own and each other's deeper vulnerable feelings, needs and wounds they were able to work things out.

## Practice

Practice connecting with your vulnerability by reaching beyond

your comfort zone. If vulnerability is difficult for you, you could do this by writing your feelings down so that you are engaging in a conversation with yourself. Or you could watch a sad movie by yourself and let yourself experience your vulnerable feelings.

Practice sharing your vulnerability. It could be something small, like giving a friend a hug if you are somebody who avoids intimacy. Or perhaps it could be simply telling someone important to you a bit more about what you are experiencing. Or you could share something that is hard for you to share. Pick a safe person in your life (not necessarily your partner). Tell that person how you feel and what you need from them (usually just listening and understanding). "I'm feeling anxious and just need you to listen to me for a few minutes." Notice if sharing like this made you feel closer to this person. If the person you shared with is safe and empathetic, you will probably feel closer to them. If they are not caring and empathetic, this will not be a nourishing experience. If you are uncomfortable with sharing your vulnerability, then it may be bringing up feelings of shame

## My Vulnerability

I grew up without any skill or knowledge about being vulnerable other than expressing my sadness by crying. As I trained to become a therapist, I learned a lot about vulnerability and revealing more of myself. Even though it was difficult, I became more and more open, and other people would show themselves to me in return. In my writing, I often share very personal and unguarded stories about my own life. The posts I write that are highly vulnerable generally get many more comments, emails, and feedback than the less vulnerable writing I do. We crave vulnerable communication because we crave "real" connections and conversations. We all want to be "real" like Rabbit. And it is easier if somebody else goes first and opens that door for us.

## The Gift of Connected Listening

You will change your relationships as you develop the ability to share and listen. Take the time to communicate directly about how you affect each other. Practice by having only one person speak while the other listens and then reflect back what you each said. Take turns. Let them know you heard what they said without arguing, defending, or doing anything other than acknowledging their truth. Pick a time when you can be free of other responsibilities. Shut off any phones and sit down facing each other. Look into their eyes. Notice your partner (or friend, relative etc.). Notice this precious being who is sitting with you. Breathe.

**She:** Would you take a few minutes and listen to me?

**He:** Sure.

**She:** I felt upset today when you were watching TV and didn't get up to greet me.

**He:** When I didn't get up to greet you when you got home, you felt upset.

**She:** Yes, it hurt my feelings and made me feel unappreciated.

**He:** My not getting up to greet you hurt your feelings, and you felt unappreciated.

**She:** Yes, I think I feel unappreciated easily and would like you to make an effort to let me know that I am important to you.

**He:** You would like me to let you know that you are important to me. That would help you feel more appreciated.

**She:** Yes. And I do appreciate you listening now and taking the time to understand. Thank you.

**He:** My taking the time to listen to you now feels good to you, and you appreciate it.

**She:** Yes.

**He:** Thank you for sharing with me. I don't want you to feel upset and as if I am ignoring you. I didn't know you felt like that.

**She:** Thank you for listening. It feels good that you listened and took my feelings seriously.


While this may not be how you usually communicate, wouldn't you love for your partner to really listen to you like this? We all need to be heard and understood without the other person explaining or defending. In the scenario above, the boyfriend did a great job of listening to his girlfriend. He didn't take her feelings personally. She had a different need, and he was there to listen and understand. Ideally, both partners will initiate the process of talking and asking the other person to listen and understand them. Over time, these partners will understand each other more deeply and develop a closer relationship.

This is part of the magic of a growing relationship. As we integrate vulnerability into who we are and how we relate, our relationships smooth out. The rough bumps become less frequent and less traumatic. We connect on a deeper level. Like the Velveteen Rabbit, our soft and worn spots make us real and lovable.

If you want to read more about connective listening, my blog posting, *"Intimacy (Into-Me-See): Invite Your Partner For A Visit Into Your World," [www.jenniferlehrmft.com/?p=255]* might be helpful for you to read.

# Chapter 13

## Ingredient Six: Insight

**I am comfortable with and understand my feelings and thoughts.**

Imagine that you have great self-understanding and a sharp intuition. You have clarity about who you are. You understand what makes you tick, and what triggers you. You are in touch with your feelings and thoughts and understand why you are having them. You understand your motivations and your beliefs.

You are able to manage your feelings: you don't push them away, and they don't hijack you. The emotions you experience and the beliefs tied to them unravel and smooth out. You are able to change your thoughts from destructive to supportive.

When you run into a conflict, you understand which wounds are getting triggered in yourself (and hopefully learn about your partner's wounds too). Your insight about your feelings serves as a guide to greater emotional intelligence, rather than your feelings being an engine that compulsively drives you. You have the ability to witness what is occurring inside of you and choose your response.

You also see others clearly and comprehend their emotional and thinking patterns. People usually can't pull the wool over your eyes because of this ability.

The events of your relationship and life make sense. You use your understanding of yourself and others to make your relationship work, and your feelings and thoughts assist you, rather than wreak havoc on your relationship. Because you have a clear vision and comprehension of yourself, you navigate through your life easily.

Your insight brings harmony into your life and relationships. This ability makes you a pleasure to be with and is another major component of a relationship-ready person.

## Self-Knowledge is a Great Navigator

When I was younger, I was pretty confused about who I was. When one of my early boyfriends asked me to marry him, I said "no" but had no idea why. Why wouldn't I want to marry him? I loved him. I was attracted to him. We were great friends. He was a great guy. This event threw me into emotional turmoil and caused me to initiate therapy for myself. I began to examine my life and, over time, grew to understand myself more.

If you pay attention to yourself and unravel your perception of your experiences (how you feel, what you think, what hurts, what is confusing, etc.), over time, you will figure a lot out about yourself. I did, and I am glad. I can't imagine being that anxious and confused young woman again. I am so *grateful* to understand myself and to truly be in command of my life.

Great relationships require that we understand our own story, including our desires, needs, and wounds. They require that we know ourselves well enough to not get pulled into the past or unrealistic scenarios or fears about our future. Our relationships need us to manage our feelings, but to in order to do that, we must know what they are and why they are being triggered. This allows us to be non-reactive and safe for our partners to be with.

It is important to have the clarity of self-knowledge and to be able to trust our own reactions and responses. If we cannot guide ourselves in our relationships because we do not know how to interpret what is occurring or do not understand ourselves, we will cause damage. It is important to become educated about who we are, who our partner is, and what a relationship is. We need self-knowledge and insight.

## How Well Do You Know Yourself?

Are you comfortable with all of your feelings? Do you understand where your thoughts come from? Do you understand your motivations and fears? When you catch yourself being judgmental

or resentful, can you understand why and see the way out?

Some people are not well developed in terms of understanding their emotions. Many others get "hijacked" by their emotions. There is little training on emotions in our world. How many of us have asked somebody, "What are you feeling?" and have gotten the reply of, "I don't know," or "Nothing"? How many of us have gotten lost in our feelings when upset? How many of us are at ease with all of our feelings?

## Don't Do This!

Recently I was privy to a situation where a relationship was coming apart. This couple had struggled with understanding each other, tolerating their differences, and getting their needs for a safe connection met. Jason would often get very upset when he felt pushed away by his girlfriend Kara. His reaction is where things went wrong. He took his disappointment and used it to blame his girlfriend. He became angry and threatening, so of course, she pulled away. He did not know how to talk about his deep feelings of hurt without blasting Kara. He could not see that his upset feelings did not give him the right to blame. Nor did he see that his sense of disappointment and hurt did not give him the right to be verbally abusive. His lack of insight and the resulting bad behavior was the lynchpin that killed this relationship. Would you want to be with someone who behaved like that? Would anyone want to be with you if you behaved like that? Probably not.

Another common scenario is to take our "bad" feelings and stuff them down in some internal dungeon instead of examining them. The trouble is, they escape and take over when you least want them to. I'm sure most of us have experienced a "feeling attack." Without looking within, we don't have the ability to do our own internal work or to develop the clarity of insight.

## Curiosity Is Your Friend

If we can allow ourselves to be curious about our feelings instead of disowning them or letting them run the show, they will begin to mature. We will then be able to understand them better and communicate them more easily. We will begin to understand not just our feelings, but also our beliefs and how we hide from ourselves. Being on good terms with this part of ourselves is essential to becoming *relationship-ready*.

Train yourself to not react but to think before you respond. Remember, if you aren't building a bridge between yourself and someone else via open and respectful communication, you may be blocking or blowing one up. Communicating a feeling is different than acting it out. Slamming a door is different than saying, "That really hurt my feelings, and I'm feeling angry with you. We need to talk." Expressing sadness or grief is different than starting an argument because of a feeling of fear and loss. "I'm sad that I have to work while you go on a fishing trip," is different than saying, "Why do you have to go? I can't believe you would do this. You are so selfish."

I used to have a good friend who would get upset at other people's driving. She behaved as if what they did was a personal affront. She would often pick me up in the morning to go to the gym together. When another driver upset her, instead of talking to me about how upset she felt, she would hit the gas and race after the car that "offended" her. She wasn't able to differentiate between her feelings and the actions she was taking. She didn't have good insight about this behavior. Needless to say, her actions didn't make me feel safe. Although I talked to her about my feelings, she was unable to hear them and unwilling to adjust her behavior.

## Learning to Look Deeper

Look at an aspect of your partner or another person you feel judgmental towards. Notice a behavior of theirs that bothers you. What is it? Why does it bother you? Now imagine that person as a small child. See that behavior as something they developed in order to feel good about themselves or survive.

For example, Mary was very controlling, and Jim couldn't stand it. What he didn't realize was that Mary grew up with an out-of-control alcoholic mother. Mary became responsible for getting her siblings to do their homework, fixing them dinner, and then getting them ready for bed. She learned to over-manage because she had to keep things going, and there was no one else to depend on. But now these skills that helped her survive drive her boyfriend nuts because she micromanages his every move. As both Mary and Jim learned about Mary's history and how that survival strategy came out of a painful time, their insight about each other and themselves grew; and they were able to make much-needed changes and become better partners to each other.

When you run into a problem, learn to talk about your differences and what they mean to each of you. Doing this will help you discover more about each other and develop more insight. But also respect those differences. You would be bored out of your mind if the person of your dreams were *exactly* the same as you. And you wouldn't have this opportunity to grow.

## Do You Understand Your Wounds?

The lack of understanding of our inner world of feelings, thinking, and beliefs often starts when we are children. One day in a parking lot, I saw a little boy crying. Instead of saying, "I'm sorry you are upset; I know you want xyz," his mother yelled at him because she was embarrassed and frustrated. That response made that little boy feel not understood, unloved and alone. He cried even harder. He had no way of dealing with his feelings about not being able to have what he wanted because his mother did not help him do that. She did not help him soothe himself and accept and understand his normal feelings of being upset. Instead, she punished him emotionally. As she yelled at him more and more, he sobbed harder and harder.

As this scenario continues over the years (and without his mother getting help and gaining insight, it will), this little boy will most likely disconnect from his deep feeling of abandonment. (His mother was abandoning him emotionally and was being emotionally abusive

to him.) He may not even remember this happening. Instead, he may believe he had a "good" childhood. And he may have thoughts connected to these emotions that he is not conscious of. He will easily feel misunderstood and probably not emotionally trust whomever he is in a relationship with. He will hide emotionally, and he won't have a good understanding of his own feelings or reactions. He won't be on good terms with many of his feelings, and he will push his needs deep inside.

Later when he's married or in a serious relationship, all of this will come flying out in a rage when his partner unintentionally triggers him, or he will cut his partner off and isolate himself. Whatever the scenario, he probably won't be able to talk about his feelings in a productive and connected way.

This story is already deep inside of him. He will have a lot of self-examination to do if he wants to make a magic cake with someone. It isn't his fault, but it is his path. If you pick him or someone like him, you will also have a lot to do. Once you move out of the "in love" phase, and the real differences surface, you will feel abandoned by his not being open with you. And he won't be able to tolerate your frustration or anger. The two of you will have to learn how to redo both of your pasts by developing the necessary ingredients.

## Is Your Sight Clear?

Here is another common scenario. Kelly had a boyfriend, Mark, but he was not committed to her. He played around with other women. Kelly eventually broke up with Mark, but several weeks later when he invited her to a hotel for a romantic evening, she jumped at the chance. Why? She was so hungry for love she wasn't seeing clearly. She didn't see that he had done nothing to change. He was just doing his thing, trying to have some fun without talking about what had gone wrong and his inability to be there for her.

Kelly's hunger was blocking her insight. She couldn't see Mark clearly, although all her friends thought he was immature and inappropriate. She also didn't see that she was so hungry for love that she would put up with all kinds of disrespectful behavior. Hopefully, she will eventually decide that seeing the truth is more important than desperately hanging on to someone who isn't relationship-ready.

Your story will be different, yet you, too, are on a journey of self-knowledge.

## What Is Your Relationship Pattern?

Imagine you are looking down at your relationship or pattern of relationships from a place way above the earth. You have a bird's eye view and can see your experiences and patterns clearly. You are watching and analyzing how you are in relationships or a particular relationship. For example, you might be noticing that you get upset because you don't feel respected by your partner and realize you need to learn you are worthy of respect.

One of my ongoing life-challenges has been and is learning to stand up for myself and speak my truth. I have had to learn to do this over and over again in numerous and various scenarios. This has been challenging for me because I tend to be afraid of being

misunderstood or even blamed or judged. Because I have the insight that this is an area where I have had and occasionally still have to practice, I don't fight it. I see the challenge, take a deep breath, and build that muscle.

Stop and think about your sense of curiosity about yourself. Think about how you relate to your feelings and thoughts. Think about what is difficult for you or confusing. Having clear vision means understanding why you feel as you do and why you think as you do. Without self-understanding, when you run into a challenge, you can dissolve into chaos, as can your relationship. Understanding the story of who you are and the experiences you have had is like stepping out of a dark room and into the light. Grab your notebook and write about your self-understanding. You can use the following questions as a guide.

Or if you prefer, skip the following questions. Instead, close your eyes and think about what you do and do not understand about yourself, life, or a relationship. Imagine that you have complete self-understanding. You might get an image or a feeling. Write about whatever comes up for you.

---

- How are your emotions your friend? How are they your enemy?
- What "pushes your buttons" and why?

- What is your part in the difficulties and challenges in your relationships?

- What are your limitations? What are your partner's?

- What works in your relationship? In your life?

- What does not work in your relationship? In your life?

---

## Do You Have These Qualities?

How do you develop insight? How do you learn to see the story that explains what is happening and why?

Developing insight is an ongoing process. There is always more to learn. There is always more to examine, explore, experience and sort through. There are a number of qualities involved in developing better insight. These include:

- **Curiosity**—Curiosity is your friend. Wanting to understand yourself is a big part of developing insight. Without curiosity, you won't ask, "Hey, how do I create my experiences; and how do I change them?"

- **Mindfulness**—Slow down and take the time to process your feelings and notice your experience. You can't develop insight if you are too busy to notice your own experience. Having a meditation or yoga practice can be a great help with this. When you practice yoga, for example, you start to notice your thoughts;

things like, "This is hard. I don't like it." Then you realize that this is what you tell yourself in other situations your life.

- **Exploration**—Learn to enjoy looking within yourself and what works and does not work in your life and relationship. Exploration is like putting together a puzzle. Actively look within and sort through your experiences, feelings, and beliefs.

- **Intuition**—It's that inner knowing. Sort through your internal voices so that you learn to differentiate between a fear voice and your intuition. Learn to listen to the little voice that "knows." When we are caught in fear, our curiosity often shuts down, and we can't access our intuition, which helps us with our insight. Intuition also helps us with magic, the final ingredient we will be looking at.

- **Desire**—There is a story about a young man who asked a master how to become enlightened. The master grabbed him and held his head under water in the river. When he let him up, he said, "Tell me, what did you want most of all when you were under water?" The young man said, "I wanted to breathe!" The master said, "When you want enlightenment (or god) that much, you will be ready." This is how important desire is. Desire is the gateway to doing what it takes to get what you wish for.

## Do You Treat Your Life Like a Garden?

Learning about yourself is a lifelong process. For me, this process is wonderful. I don't want my psyche to be a chaotic mess. I want to understand, organize, and beautify my inner world. It is as if we are each a garden. As we tend to and learn about ourselves, we develop the tools to make our garden beautiful. For me, knowing myself is a significant way I create beauty in my life. Creating isn't just about making pictures and objects; we actually create our lives. As your self-understanding increases, you create a more and more amazing you and develop the potential to create a more fulfilling relationship.

Start to look at yourself and your life as a beautiful creation. You are the artist. You have the opportunity to create your thoughts and your attitudes. You get to create how you see the world. You can choose to be kind or unkind, patient or impatient, loving or cruel. You can choose to treat yourself well or punish yourself. You get to decide who you want to be. You can be someone you would want to be with—or not.

Try this affirmation, "I choose to create love and beauty in my life."

Choose to develop your mindfulness. Choose to develop your curiosity. Choose to explore. Choose to develop your intuition. Activate your desire. And tell yourself, "I want to do it all in this life. I want to be the most I can be. I want to live a beautiful life and have a beautiful relationship, and the way to start is with self-understanding."

## Will You Dig Down Deep?

Affirmations are valuable because when we focus on them, they

bring up the parts of ourselves that do not believe them. Those parts want to be explored and healed. There is a huge difference between focusing on the positive because we believe it and pretending that we believe something positive we do not believe deep down. We develop insight as we delve down and explore the many aspects of our emotional and thinking selves.

I was recently struggling with some health issues, and there seemed to be an emotional component. When my therapist asked me to affirm, "I do not need to be sick for others," I had a moment of sadness. I had an image of my father being upset at me when I was a child. I realized my father had resented taking care of us because he felt like he didn't have enough for himself, and that this was affecting my belief that I *deserved* to be well. I was still carrying this emotional wound. As a child, it was easier for me to believe that I didn't deserve than it was to believe that my father was not always good to me because of his own demons.

I decided I wasn't going to continue to take on my father's negativity and resentment. I decided I did not want this old belief in my life. Identifying this inner emotional wound and deciding I didn't want to believe it anymore allowed the unconscious part of me that didn't know if she deserved to be well and taken care of to shift. This is how we can heal deep, underlying beliefs that harm us.

## A Writing Exercise

Use my example above as a guide to this exercise.

- Think about something that is difficult for you.

- See if you can find a positive affirmation of what you wish for around that issue.

- Then imagine yourself as a child.

- See if any thoughts or feelings come up that help you understand when and why that issue developed.

- What were you struggling with? What was going on that was hurtful?

- How did this belief help you?

- Are you ready to let go of that belief or struggle?

- Write an affirmation to counter that old belief.

As you identify the issue and choose to let it go, you are increasing your insight and healing yourself. You are shifting your underlying beliefs.

As you continue to explore who you are and why you are the way you are, your insight will grow. Your insight will shine like a light through confusion and clutter. This clarity will help you to manifest the relationship of your dreams.

If you want to read more about the work required to develop insight, read my blog post, *"Inside and Out."* [*www.jenniferlehrmft. com/?p=756]*

# Chapter 14

## Ingredient Seven: Magic

**My path is magic.**

I love magic. I've always loved magic—not the magician tricks kind, but the magic of a sunset, a piece of poetry or music, or a little kitten or puppy. Or the magic of a happy ending or a dream that comes true. I especially love the magic that comes from having the power to influence our own reality in ways beyond our expectations.

My experience with magic started early. My father was an artist and illustrator, and when I was a child, I use to watch him paint. I watched the blank, white canvas slowly become a scene: a picture with colors, light and shadow, cities and skies, atmosphere

and dimension. That was where I learned first about the magic of creating. Anything could be created. Anything was possible. From nothing, these beautiful images emerged. That was a long time ago, and much has changed for me since then. The magic I care about now is not the magic of making a beautiful picture, but the magic of making a beautiful life and relationship. I've been learning, practicing, and perfecting that for many years. Despite the aspects of my life that are difficult or challenging, much of my life is magical. I *know* we are the creators of our perceptions and lives.

## Magic Is Essential

Imagine living a life of synchronicity and magic. As you see and accept the magic of your path, you trust that every challenge and difficult moment has a gift in it. You trust your intuition and feel guided. You trust you are on the "yellow-brick road" to your heart's desires. With each step you take, the perfect path materializes in front of you. You see each moment as an opportunity to be lived authentically and with grace. You easily prioritize your choices because it is clear what is most important at each moment. This allows you to love freely and easily. This allows you to follow your dreams.

You understand what your relationship is asking of you, how it is challenging you, and what it is teaching you. You know that learning to love means becoming whole. You look for meaning and intention in all you encounter, and as you find it, you engage and cooperate with your life and partner fully.

# Ingredient Seven: Magic

You are a magician. You can fully claim your power to create a life that shimmers with intention, beauty, and true love. Ultimately, this allows you to manifest someone you love who feels lucky to have you and deserves you.

## Where Is Your Magic?

We live in a fast-paced and materialistic world. We are taught to focus on the external, whether it is the right job, the right house, the right college, etc. There is not a strong focus on life as a process of learning and growing. There is not a strong focus on our inner lives. There is very little understanding of magic or synchronicity or how to have grace in our lives. This handicaps us, for we may lose perspective when we hit a difficult time. Instead of understanding what is being asked of us, we may feel bad about ourselves or angry at life.

I have had countless difficult times in my life. While I'm in them, I may feel afraid, overwhelmed, or sorry for myself. Yet once I accept that there is something I must overcome, accomplish, or change, I apply myself. When I have passed through this challenge, I find that I have new skills and strengths. I continue forward with these earned gifts (they weren't for free) less encumbered.

Sometimes we choose to do something difficult—like put ourselves through college while working. We may feel as if we are a tiny tree in a forest. We can see the sky way above, but it takes

time, persistence, and focus to grow into the big tree who can feel the sun on her branches as they reach into the sky. Once we make the choice to do this, we have taken on a challenge that will make us grow, despite the difficulty.

If we don't understand the deep learning being asked, we may feel ashamed of our situation as if life is about winning or getting the prize. This sets us up to be frustrated or angry and causes us to swim upstream and lose our connection to our own magic. Because of the lack of focus on and understanding of magic and the bigger perspective, we can get stuck. We can tell ourselves things are not okay, or nothing is right. This is a destructive place to be.

Challenges provide us with something to learn. This learning will contribute to having a better life. Like the Buddhist monk who meditates to create a clearer awareness or the painter who learns to create increasingly beautiful pictures, we, too, can bring more and more clarity, beauty, magic, and love into our lives.

Magic isn't about fantasy. It is about the profound interconnection and intentionality of our path and our experiences, and it is what allows doors to open as we engage deeply with our lives and ourselves.

## Magic, Karma, and Manifestation

The concept of magic can be confusing. We can feel stuck in our lives. How do we find magic? What is it? How does it relate to karma?

## Ingredient Seven: Magic

How does it relate to manifestation? This is a complicated area, and I can only tell you my understanding of it. For me, it is as if I am on a journey. Each event in my life has a purpose and contributes to my soul's growth. Karma is the actual path, the rocks, the easy spots, the steepness or gentleness of the terrain. Manifestation comes from my will. I desire to walk this path, and I apply myself. As my will and my karma interact, my path teaches me and changes. Each step or interaction causes a new scenario to develop. The path opens up organically. As I engage in my life with more honesty, clarity, and good faith, the magic becomes more beautiful. My early life was significantly more difficult than my present life. The magic was harder to see, but it was there, for it was the path from then to now.

## The Gift of Our Challenges

Here is an example of how the gifts of our challenges often aren't apparent until much later.

Rosy had a difficult first marriage. Her husband Bill wasn't emotionally available. She tried to cuddle up to him, but he acted uninterested. It seemed that he would rather watch TV or play on the computer. While Rosy yearned for a connected relationship, she ended up focusing on her career. She went back to school, got a degree, and started a successful business. Rosy and Bill never were able to work it out. They ended up divorcing.

Four years later, Rosy married again. Her next marriage was to

Charles. Charles was a sweet and loving man, and Rosy was very happy. She was happy to have her career, too. She also had a child in this marriage. She had it all.

Years later, she realized that had she been happy in her first marriage, she never would have gone back to school and developed her career. She realized that one of her lessons was to be more independent, and she loved the independent part of herself. She also realized that developing her career made her feel strong enough to leave her first marriage. She realized that Charlie was a much better father than Bill would have been. Looking back, it all made sense, even though while she was in the pain of her first marriage, nothing made sense. She had felt like she was being punished.

If you were to ask Rosy, she would tell you she would do it all again. Rosy knew that she didn't have the capacity to pick the "right" man earlier in her life. But that relationship inadvertently pushed her to develop herself. And what she learned allowed her to pick a much more compatible person the second time around. As difficult as it was, the rewards she received were worth it. She learned what she needed in that first situation to make her life much better later.

It is easy to appreciate the times that are nourishing, but it is more difficult to accept the challenges. It is important to cooperate and engage with the intention of our relationships, even during the difficult times. In order to do this, we must understand what is being asked of us, both by our lives as well as by our relationships. And we must trust that as we cooperate and engage fully with our lives, we have stepped onto the path of magic—even if in the moment it doesn't feel so magical.

We may not have been taught to see magic or to understand what is important. We may not have been taught to persevere or continue even when our life is difficult. We may not understand that as our challenges and imperfections arise, they guide us to the next step we need to take to become a better person and partner.

We may not understand that as we live out the integrity of finding our best and most relational selves, our lives do change. As we practice this over and over, we *do* create wonderful relationships. We do find happiness. We do come to recognize and experience the magic of our lives.

## Your Magic

Are the purposes of the events of your life clear or unclear? Sometimes our lives throw us a curve ball and ask a lot of us. We may have to learn something we don't want to learn. Sometimes the purpose of our relationship or a chapter in our lives is clear; sometimes it is not so clear. Sometimes we choose partners we need, but don't necessarily want or who can't fully be there for us. We may not recognize the learning this partnership or event will catalyze. Say, "yes" to this challenge; claim your magic and become the magician who has it all: a true love and a beautiful life.

Grab your notebook and write about the magic of your life. You can use the following questions as a guide.

Or if you prefer, skip the following questions. Instead, close your eyes and think about magic. Imagine a magical life. You might get an image or a feeling. Write about whatever comes up for you.

---

- Do you trust your intuition and the synchronicities of your life?

- What synchronicities have occurred in your life?

- How have past challenges helped you gain more magic in your life?

- What does your relationship need from you, or what is it teaching you?

- What are you learning now that will enable you to create more purpose, intention, and capacity to self-actualize in your life or a relationship?

- How are you being asked to stretch? What are your opportunities for growth?

- What challenge would you like to take on that may eventually open up more magic in your life?

---

## Claiming Your Magic

How do we step into the realm of magic? How do we bring magic into our relationship?

We have to accept that our lives have a purpose. We have to see our life as our friend. We have to know that as we work on being our best selves, our life will cooperate with us. Seeing our life as something we cooperate with, rather than fight against, will move us from going against the flow to going with it. Once we are cooperating with our life and open to what it wants to teach us, our experience of magic increases.

The path of magic includes the ability to appreciate our lives and also to find meaning in each moment. We need to know that our lives matter and have purpose. We cannot thrive if we do not have meaning, and our relationships cannot flourish if they do not have purpose. That purpose could be working together, having children, being a family together, experiencing love and support, learning something together, gaining new perspectives, overcoming a specific challenge, sharing a vision or a dream, or even something else. Sometimes we are asked to grow. Sometimes we have to learn patience, kindness, or firmness. Or we may have to overcome a fear that impacts our relationship or ourselves. Embracing what our lives are asking of us is part of stepping into our magic.

Personally, some of the lessons I have had were about allowing my partner to be who he was, even if he could not meet my needs. At the same time, I had to find my own boundaries about what I

would or would not tolerate. I also had to focus on and develop my own life independent of my partner.

For example, when I had a boyfriend with addiction issues, I learned I could not make him stop using. The trap of trying to make this person different drained a lot of opportunity for experiencing magic in my life. As I learned to disengage from his problem, I gained more freedom and magic in my life. This lesson was a long and complex one for me because it coexisted with learning to ask for what I needed and to not accept what was not good enough. It is a lesson that took different forms in different relationships.

Over time, I learned both that my partner is different and has his or her own growth curve and lessons, and that I could ask for what I desired. This is particularly tricky when what I wanted could not happen because my partner had his own learning to do. Having patience and holding a long view is important when dealing with this kind of a challenge.

I developed the other ingredients too—creating my own sense of safety, not taking too much responsibility for someone else, following my dreams, finding a sense of caring even when I was hurt or disappointed, learning how to be vulnerable, and understanding my internal world. By integrating all of these ingredients, I was able to claim the magic of my path.

After I had gained many skills from my previous relationships, I was ready for a different kind of relationship. I had developed enough relationship-ready qualities that I was ready for someone who could grow with me in a more complete way. I had done enough inner work. I was ready for a relationship that could more fully meet both of our needs.

Remember, whatever happens to you has a lesson and is asking you to develop some quality that enables either you or your relationship to improve. Each relationship is unique with very specific areas that feel good, and very specific areas that are difficult. These relationship challenges force us to stretch and grow.

The question to ask is, "What is the intention of this situation or this relationship, and how do I best engage with it?" How I engage with each situation allows or blocks the possibility of magic. As you think in this way, you will stop fighting whatever your life is handing you, and your magic path will open.

## Trusting Your Magic

How do you live with such trust that you know that as you take each step, the perfect experience materializes under your feet? Manifestation starts with envisioning what you want. Sit down and imagine what the perfect relationship would look like for you. Do not imagine the externals, like if they look like a movie star, but instead focus on the internal, such as the qualities of love and togetherness that you desire.

When we imagine our "dream person," we often focus on the feeling of being loved and merging. We often do not focus on qualities. Try thinking about qualities such as wisdom, patience,

generosity, kindness, or the ability to connect, or communicate etc. Being with a selfish person will feel much different than being with a generous person. And you will find that these qualities are much more important than external details.

Imagine how you would like to feel in this relationship. Let yourself dream. Sometimes we have to bring into our imagination what we want to manifest before it can occur. There was a time when I watched a particular romantic movie over and over again—so many times I would be embarrassed to guess. I didn't know why at the time; I was just incredibly drawn to this movie and the sense of closeness and happiness it depicted. Later I figured out I was imprinting that sense of togetherness into me (which I didn't have much experience with) so that I could manifest a great relationship with a lot of closeness. And that's just what I did.

Write down the qualities you desire in your relationship and that you, hopefully, embody as well. Describe what you long for. Then ask yourself if there is anything in you that is blocking this. See if anything comes to you. It may be you are with somebody who isn't growing or isn't capable of giving you what you need. It may be you don't believe it is possible or believe you don't deserve it. It may be that you and your partner just need to roll up your sleeves and gain some new tools, or it could be something else. Write about whatever you believe may be blocking you from this relationship. As you write about it, you are starting the process of unblocking yourself.

Don't let yourself get dejected if it feels like you can't make it happen. Nothing changes in an instant. Everything takes time. Trust that as you ask for what you want, life will bring in the experiences you need to help you grow and manifest that desire. You only need to be open to your desires and engage with them. You are a powerful and magical being. You have everything you need to become relationship-ready and change your life.

For a short article on developing more magic in your life, read my blog post, *"What If I Decided My Life Is My Friend?" [www. jenniferlehrmft.com/?p=246]*

# Chapter 15

## The Relationship-Ready You

Congratulate yourself! You've covered a lot of ground. You are more relationship-ready than ever. You probably have new insights about yourself and about relationships. You have an entire new shelf of ingredients in your pantry, ready to use as you make your magic cake.

Don't worry that some of these ingredients may feel new or challenging. As you focus on them, they will grow and expand—which is what the tools of desire, intention, manifestation, and magic are all about.

You may have already realized that these seven ingredients are integrated. They overlap and interact with each other. As you feel safer, you will have a better relationship with your feelings. As you learn to have empathy for yourself and your partner, you will have an easier time with vulnerable communication. As you become more empowered, you will see the purpose of your relationship. As you love and respect yourself, your sense of self-esteem increases. As you trust in the magic of your path, you feel safer . . . and on and on.

Start wherever you feel most called. As you focus in one area, the other areas will grow, too. You will continue to gain skill and make these ingredients better and better. This is part of the magic of manifestation.

As you become more and more relationship-ready, manifesting your true love might happen quickly; or it might be a longer, slower process like it was for me. Whatever the case, enjoy the journey and make each moment of your life as beautiful as you can.

If you have a partner, you are probably thinking about whether the two of you can jump up to the relational mixing bowl together to make your magic cake—maybe you already have.

If you and your partner haven't been able to smooth out your relationship, you may be thinking about why and what to do about it. For more help, my online system WeConcile®—"Help for Committed Couples Seeking Help," will walk you and your partner through your relationship difficulties and guide you in creating your perfect relationship step by step. You can learn more at *www. Jenniferlehrmft.com/weconcile/*.

You can also read either of my two blogs: My personal blog (*Jennifer's Blog—www.jenniferlehrmft.com/?p=1430*) where I share my personal experiences or my **Healing Tips Blog [www. jenniferlehrmft.com/?p=1432]** where I share tips on healing our relationships and ourselves. They are both here: **www. JenniferLehrmft.com**.

If you are really struggling, get support or find a therapist. Nothing is better than having a trained, impartial third party help you sort through your difficulties. Relationships can be problematic and painful, but they can also be graceful and beautiful. Believe that you can get through the hard stuff and make yours wonderful.

If you are single and still searching for your true love, keep learning about yourself and growing. You'll be that much more relationship-ready when you meet your dream person. Your walk down relationship lane will be smoother and easier, less rocky and treacherous.

Finally, if you are in a relationship but suspect you should leave, it might be helpful to read my blog post, **"When to Hold and When to Fold."** *[www.jenniferlehrmft.com/?p=523]*

No matter what, don't let go of your dreams. We all deserve love, respect, and support. We deserve happiness and joy.

As you continue on this path of self-growth, you will gain the skills you need to manifest a happy life for yourself. Your relationship with yourself will become more beautiful. This will allow you to manifest a great relationship. You will be an example to others of what is possible. Your own happiness will contribute to increasing happiness for everyone.

As more and more people learn the skills needed to manifest their wondrous relationship, those skills will flow over into other areas: parenting, work relationships, friendships, manifesting our dreams, etc. As each person becomes more and more relationship-ready, all of our relationships will be more peaceful. Our world will become more peaceful. Divorce rates will decrease. Children will be better nurtured because parents in more supportive relationships are more stable, balanced and healthier.

We will become a community of people who support and help each other more and more, and inflict wounds on each other less and less. We will become a world that has greater connection and respect for all the forms of life and love on this planet. We will care about our impact on others. We will see the magic of the clouded leopard in the rainforest and the specialness of our own puppy. And we will look into the eyes of the person across from us with a curious and grateful heart. You are part of this path of the blossoming of light and love. I'm excited for you and hope you are excited for yourself. May your path be magical and filled with love and bliss.

# Acknowledgments

Writing a book is a journey. Along the way, others provided nourishment in the way of encouragement, editing, and feedback.

My husband Michael Bosworth is always encouraging and supportive of my many projects. He is the amazing man with whom I am making a magic cake. I am ever grateful for his love and his desire to connect fully and deeply with me. And he is gracious enough to not mind being in some of the examples in this book.

Thanks to Michele Khoury for her feedback including pointing out my over use of "that" and "actually." That was a major revelation in itself. My sister-in-law Wendy Bosworth took the first real crack at editing and also was the first person to say, "I like it." Thanks for your support. A number of other people also provided very useful feedback. One of those was Marilyn Faulkner, who helped me see

how to get some air into the batter, so the cake wasn't too dense. Thank you all.

All of my past relationships have informed my growth. These include teachers, therapists, friends, partners, and family members. Thank you to each of you who contributed to my life challenges, learning and deeper understanding of love. Thank you also to all the pets I've known who have blessed me with absolute and complete unconditional love. For them, I am extremely grateful. They made my early life survivable, and they make my current life more joyful. Finally, I thank the creative force of life itself, in all of its forms and presences. Without an alignment to the principals of truth, love, and peace, no growth or magic would be possible.

# About The Author

You might want to know a little bit about me. Personal transformation has been my focus for many decades. I'm also a licensed marriage and family therapist in addition to being an author. You can find my history of transformation and training in a story: *"The Little Black Bag." [www.jenniferlehrmft.com/?p=922]*

As a child, I loved books, animals, and anything creative. As I grew up and followed a creative path, it became clear to me that despite facility in the areas of art and creativity, I wasn't good at standing up for myself or taking care of myself in relationship to others. I found myself unable to be fully empowered, and after a particularly difficult relationship, I hit bottom emotionally.

Reevaluating my priorities, I began to focus on a variety of learning, meditations, teachings, workshops, and therapy. I wanted

more than anything to have full ownership of myself, to be able to walk through the world without fear and in full possession of my value as a human and spiritual being. As a result, my life has been focused on personal transformation, growth and relationship health for many years. This focus has become what my life is about and is now what I continue to value and learn, as well as give back to the world. I have integrated the experiences I have gained navigating life's challenges into my work: my clinical skills and my writing. I love assisting others in moving from pain or frustration to greater empowerment, satisfying relationships, and joyful lives.

Social Media is a good way to connect, if you are interested. I often create helpful couples' quotes on **Pinterest [www.pinterest. com/jenniferlehrmft/]** and put them on some of the other Social Media sites as well.

You can also find me on **Google+ [plus.google.com/+Jennife rLehrJenniferLehrMFT/about]**, **Facebook [www.facebook.com/ JenniferlehrMFT]**, and **Twitter [twitter.com/JenniferLehrMFT]**.

WeConcile also has social media links. We expect it to be launched and ready for beta users in the spring or summer of 2015. You can learn more about it now at either **www.weconcile.com** or through my website at **www.Jenniferlehrmft.com/weconcile/**.

23928778R00089

Made in the USA
San Bernardino, CA
04 September 2015